52 Weekly Mantras to Break
Chains, Cycles, & Ceilings

CHECK UP
FROM YOUR
NECK UP
Volume Two

MARIE HELTON TRIPLETT

In the words of Snoop Dogg, I'd like to thank ME for this book. I'd like to thank me for surviving the unthinkable, thank me for facing my demons, thank me for not giving up, thank me for choosing to heal, thank me for being courageous enough to talk about it, and thank me for putting pen to paper for others.

And I want to thank YOU for taking this step, thank you for being brave, thank you for trusting yourself, thank you for investing in your future, and thank you for loving yourself enough to choose YOU.

INTRODUCTION

At the beginning of 2020, my spirit called me to write another book, but there was one BIG problem—my anxiety screamed HELL NO. This battle raged on for most of the year, a calling on my heart swiftly shut down by my anxiety, lack of self-worth, and doubts saying I was a one-hit wonder.

Writing a book, I have discovered, is not unlike having a baby. You grow the idea inside you and it culminates with a huge amount of labor and pushing to birth it into the world. And, just like having a baby, you can get amnesia about how hard labor and delivery was. That amnesia is why women have more babies and it's why, with time, I have decided to write another book.

I worried my second book would not have the same deep insight as my first book because the first one was 38 years of powerful life lessons rolled into a greatest-hits album. How could I possibly have 52 MORE lessons to share? Well, as you know, 2020 revealed itself and may go down as one of the worst years in history.

Wildfires, racial injustice, riots, a deadly pandemic, toilet paper shortages, lockdowns, virtual learning, and one of the ugliest political races I have ever seen ended up laying the foundation for my next 52 nuggets. Even as I am writing this introduction in 2021, Texas has frozen over and most of the state is in crisis due to power outages. The world has been flipped upside down, and this book was forged in the fire of it all.

There have been unspeakable amounts of death and devastation over the last one and half years which cannot be glossed over. We lost icons like Kobe Bryant, Chadwick Boseman, Sean Connery, Little Richard, Alex Trebek, Ruth Bader Ginsburg, and John Lewis. You could not turn on the TV or open any social media site without hearing about another brutal murder or mass shootings in the streets of our cities.

We watched in horror as George Floyd was mercilessly choked to death for all to see, and let's not forget Ahmaud Arbery, Breonna Taylor, Patrick Warren Sr., Frederick Cox, and Jonathan Price, to name a few.

If that was not enough to break your spirit, closer to home we've lost grandparents, parents, children, siblings, neighbors, and friends to COVID-19 with current death tolls of more than 500,000 in the United States alone. That is over a half-million families grieving, many of whom were robbed of proper goodbyes because of lockdown restrictions.

I am not bringing this up simply for a stroll down memory lane, but because whether you realize it or not, most of us are suffering from a case of PTSD (post-traumatic stress disorder) from the events of the last year. One thing I am very familiar with is trauma. I also know how easy it is to get stuck in a state of hypervigilance, a sense of waiting for the next shoe to drop, holding your breath in anticipation of the next catastrophe. We are not designed to stay in this high-stress state, and I hope that in these pages you will find some insight to help you unpack all the baggage that you brought with you into this year.

If you are looking for a politely assembled list of clichés, this isn't it. These mantras will challenge you to get messy, peel back layers, and walk straight into many of the things you are avoiding. You cannot glamorize the healing process and certainly cannot make things go back to the way they were, but you can collect the broken pieces to rebuild a new version of yourself, one week at a time. Today we begin a journey together that has unfettered potential, and this is both terrifying and empowering. The question is not who are you, but who do you want to be?

WEEK 1

BLIND REJECTION

Many people have heard of the term blind acceptance, I talked about it in my last book and frequently think about how it applies in my own life. For those of you new to the concept, blind acceptance is the willingness to take on beliefs without doing any research or study on the subject. Often because we trust the people sharing the information or because it has always been done that way, we just go along with it.

The reason blind acceptance is dangerous is that it puts others in a position of authority when it comes to our core beliefs and, knowing all humans have biases and agendas, leaves us vulnerable to being manipulated. As I've been on my growth journey and reflecting on blind acceptance, I realized there is a sister concept to blind acceptance that is equally detrimental to our growth—a term I have coined blind rejection.

A simple way to explain blind rejection is what happens when you set a plate of Brussels sprouts in front of a four-year-old. Instantly, without tasting them, the child will reject the plate. These could be the most delicious Brussels sprouts ever made, but the child will adamantly refuse them. I think it is normal for children to reject things without understanding them because they are children and their brains are still forming.

Some people don't grow out of this way of being. An example of how blind rejection plays out in adults is what I have noticed as a yoga teacher. Some people will never try yoga. They'll say things like "Yoga is for chicks," or "I need a *real* workout, not just stretching," or "I'm not into that foo-foo shit." There are even denominations of Christianity that have deemed yoga to be a sin of the devil.

These people will never understand the transformative powers of the practice because they have blindly rejected it. This isn't the only place I have noticed blind rejection. In my own life, I have found several places where I practiced blind rejection. The first was in receiving compliments.

When someone would extend a compliment to me, I would immediately reject their statement as if it were unbelievable. Then I would do one of two things. First, I would reciprocate the compliment with a compliment, as if I owed the person something. This behavior allowed me to shift the attention from me back to them. Second, and decidedly worse, I would call attention to my imperfections. "Oh, you think I am pretty? Have you seen my crooked dolphin toe?"

Doing the latter made me feel like I was balancing the scales. This habit formed from being told I shouldn't get too big for my britches. The elders in my life planted seeds that loving yourself was conceited and as a result of blindly accepting that belief, I subsequently rejected all compliments so I didn't appear full of myself.

Another area where I noticed this in my own life was when it came to asking for and/or receiving help. I would have rather cut off my arm than ask someone to help me. All offers to help would be promptly dismissed and I might even have given you a disgusted face for good measure. In circumstances when I had to receive help, I would beat myself up for days on end.

In both of these scenarios, I was blindly rejecting things that were good for me. The real problem with blind rejection is that the more you reject something, the less you will get of it. Think of the story about the man who drowned after rejecting three lifeboats sent to save him.

How much of my struggle could have been eased if I was more willing to accept the help when it was offered? I think about how much harder I made my life by rejecting the very things that were sent to help me. I always have to learn things the hard way.

As with all things, once you start pulling at the thread of awareness, the seams come apart. The first time someone said I should become a yoga teacher, I rejected it. The first time someone said I should write a book, I scoffed. The first time someone suggested I could make six figures—well, you get the point.

Now that I can recognize the pattern of behavior within myself I have to work actively to sit with new ideas. I have to challenge old thought patterns and commit to moving in alignment. Because I found it prevalent in my own life, I knew this had to be shared with you.

The work this week is to notice areas in your life where you may be practicing blind rejection. How is it hurting your growth and keeping you from tapping into your higher self?

There may even be ideas in this book you are tempted to disregard because they go against what you've always known. I challenge you to notice those dismissive feelings, sit with them, and determine if you are practicing blind rejection here. Beliefs propelled by wisdom will always be stronger than beliefs propelled by complacency.

Did you notice any blind
rejection this week?

_____
_____
_____
_____
_____
_____

How did it make you feel?

_____
_____
_____
_____
_____
_____

WEEK 2

F-BOMB

Right before the nationwide shutdown, I was able to take a family vacation to the Bahamas. This time, I told myself, I am going parasailing. I've always wanted to go parasailing but every trip we'd taken previously, it never worked out. I was adamant this time it would happen.

As the day approached, I mentioned it again to the whole family and no one wanted to do it with me, so I was preparing to do it alone. I asked my husband again the morning of and his answer was the same. NO! He doesn't do amusement parks, water slides, Ferris wheels, or carousels. He doesn't even like flying that much, so I knew I couldn't push it.

When we arrived at the tiki hut to sign me up for parasailing, there was only one time slot left and the lady told us it was tandem, meaning I could not go up alone. Making it worse, there was only one spot left so if I got out of the line to go find a friend to join me, someone else could sign up for it. Disappointment started to wash over me, and I think my husband could see it in my eyes.

I felt like a kid that just had their balloon popped. Realizing I was going to miss out on something that I wanted, my husband said, "Okay, fine, I'll suck it up and I'll go with you." My jaw dropped. Ya'll, he is the real MVP for this one.

He REALLY did not want to go but was willing to suffer if it meant I was happy. I could see his anxiety was building and for the next hour, while we waited for our time slot, he sipped his bourbon and tried to prepare to tackle a huge fear. "You owe me big," he kept saying.

As we loaded up onto the boat, we realized there would be several couples joining us, and I am thankful they did. We were the last couple to go, and it gave my husband a tiny bit of peace seeing all the other couples come down safely.

The guide motioned for us to get into the harness. I could see my husband white-knuckling the handlebar in terror—there was no going back. Our feet lifted off the boat and within seconds we were hundreds of feet off the earth. Adrenaline surged and my heart started to race. I was checking something off my bucket list and the excitement felt like magic.

Immediately I noticed it wasn't at all like I imagined it would be. You know how when you're on a boat, you feel like you're in a wind tunnel and it's loudly blowing in your ears so you can't hear anything over the loud sound of the wind? I thought that was what parasailing would be like, but it's not.

When you get up into the air, it's dead silent. You can't hear anything at all. I was awestruck by the whole event; you can see miles of ocean that collide into the sky along the horizon. You can see down into the crystal water with fish swimming. We could see the whole island with everybody from our cruise ship having fun. We could see the beach party and some people paddleboarding near the shoreline.

It was pure bliss for me, but what about Mike...? And before I could ask him, he looked at me and he said, "Thank you for making me do this."

Hold the freaking phone—not only did he love it, but he wanted to go again! He almost F-bombed all over my dream. We often think an F-bomb is a polite way to talk about cussing, but I use "F-bomb" to describe what happens when fear pops in—the power it has to blow up our lives. Fear is paralyzing and all-consuming.

We let fear stop us from doing things and taking action in our lives. Some fears are rational, like fear of snakes or fear of death, but most of the F-bombs are fear of failure, fear of mistakes, and fear of rejection. These are irrational fears that take up a lot of space in our lives and result in many of us living small, insignificant lives.

What if we can become students of our fear? What if we could start asking, why am I feeling this way? When was the first time I felt this fear? It is like shining the light under the bed. The boogey man under the bed can only live there until you shine the light under the bed and see that it's not real. I heard someone say once that fear is just a poor use of our imagination.

How can we retrain the brain to not be afraid? First, acknowledge fear is just emotional energy. All emotions—fear, joy, anger, resentment, happiness, and peace—are all energies. If we can harness that energy, it can work to the betterment of ourselves. The physiological response to the excitement is almost identical to fear. Your heart starts racing, your breath starts to get rapid, your stomach starts to churn. Excitement and fear feel like the exact same thing.

So if we can start rebranding our fear to excitement, then we can harness that energy, the same way we've harnessed gasoline. Gasoline, used properly, can fuel your car and put rockets into space. Used improperly, it is going to blow you up, the same as a bomb. Are you harnessing that energy and using it for your good, or are you letting it blow you up? Fear is important.

We have our fears to protect us. The limbic part of our brain, the fight-or-flight mechanism, is there to stop us from doing things that would hurt us, but too often we let it take control, and then it stops us from doing everything else as well. I'm feeling this fear because I know I'm growing. I'm feeling this way because I know I'm pushing my boundaries and I'm trying something I never thought I could.

Parasailing is scary. You're flying over the ocean and there are sharks. But, as my husband learned, on the other side of the fear was one of the most magical moments we have ever experienced together. The problem with most of us is we rely on outside encouragement that often isn't there. We must be that person in our own lives encouraging us to push beyond the things that are limiting us. We must be that person in our own lives that push beyond the things that are limiting us. The number one thing limiting you from living your best life is your fear.

One foot in front of the other, one baby step at a time, that's how you build confidence and courage in your life. I didn't just wake up courageous. I've taken little steps along the path that has made me brave, that has made me willing to go in to do whatever I need to do. I don't care what it is.

I'm willing to try anything at this point. Standing up on stage, parasailing. I still haven't quite convinced myself to go skydiving, but you get where I'm going with this. You must be the advocate in your own life, and it starts by being a student of your fear. Learn from your fear and stop letting it blow up your life.

What are you afraid of?

_____

_____

_____

_____

_____

How does fear restrict your life?

_____

_____

_____

_____

_____

WEEK 3

GREY MATTER

Ever feel like a shit human being? If not, count yourself lucky, because I do. All. The. Time. Not kidding. I am always saying something offensive, sticking my foot in my mouth, forgetting birthdays, and/or being insensitive. I can't even recycle like a good person.

Our recycling guy stopped me one week and informed me that if I didn't stop putting contaminated items in the recycling, they would end our service. If that wasn't bad enough, he proceeded to get out and check our bin before loading it. For weeks, I would hide in the curtains, holding my breath, hoping we passed the inspection. I am trying to do a better job, but I realize I have a long way to go.

It was no surprise when shortly after, my algorithm on TikTok started pushing out cleaning and organizing videos. Recently, I have been following a travel blogger who has moved from South Carolina to Japan. She has opened her world to show an American transitioning to living in a foreign country. It has been fascinating to see her experiences with how they live in Japan, but even more so to see ihow dramatically different it is from ours.

I watched her video on their seven-bin recycling system and was left scratching my head. I don't even know what goes in my single recycling bin. Not only do I feel attacked but also very confused. I had never even considered the idea that more than one recycling bin would be appropriate.

My first reaction was to reject the Japanese way—one bin is the right way, and they are wrong. A little nagging voice whispered, "Are they, though?"

A few mouse clicks later and I learned that many items that get dropped in single-stream bins become "contaminated" from the moment they fall in the bin: paper gets dirty and therefore not reusable, and glass breaks and cannot be sorted out. The cost of reprocessing increases at sorting centers, because of all the weeding out of materials that aren't usable. Due to these issues, the Container Recycling Institute claims that only 75 tons of every 100 tons collected from a single-stream recycling facility gets recycled, with the other 25 tons ending up in landfills.

Not only is the way I have been doing it my entire life less effective and more costly, but it is not even close to the best way to do it. Why did I assume Japan was wrong? That's a tough one to chew on. Many of us have been reciting the Pledge of Allegiance since we could say our ABCs and, as a veteran, I also have offered my life to support the success of the nation. I thought we recycled better out of biases, plain and simple. After all, 'merica, am I right?

I truly believe we have the potential to be the best country. I also can honestly say that we are not there yet. There are some broken systems we need to fix. Contrary to some beliefs, asking for change is not unpatriotic. It's the most patriotic thing you can do to actually try to make our country better.

You can't make improvements if you don't first acknowledge that you need to. It reminds me a lot of being a homeowner. Over time systems degrade; they get overused and backed up. If your sink starts leaking it might not be a big deal at first, but untreated, it could cause mold and water damage, eventually making the home uninhabitable. Even the best roofing will eventually need to be replaced. And, just like homeownership, there is a long honey-do list.

The answer lies in the grey area of it all and that is an uncomfortable place for many. Our brains don't like the unknown. The brain is designed to think, and prefers dealing in absolutes. That is why everything has to be labeled right or wrong, left or right, good or bad, black or white.

This linear way of thinking limits our ability to problem-solve. It can lead to division and breakdowns in communication. The grey area is where the magic is. This week, pay attention to your absolute ways of thinking.

How often do you use words like always and never?

_____

_____

_____

_____

_____

Can you be more flexible in your ways of thinking?

_____

_____

_____

_____

_____

WEEK 4

TRAINING DAYS

Go back in time with me to April 2020. What was going on in your life? Did you lose anyone in the pandemic? Were you locked up in the shutdown, missing friends and family, or maybe you lost your job and were worried about your financial future? Chances are you were in the thick of it, like the rest of the world. Grief, sadness, anxiety, and fear were the emotional cocktail we were all sipping.

Whether you realize it or not, 2020 was a training ground, and if you didn't learn anything about yourself, your priorities, and your support systems, you weren't paying attention. I know a lot of people who finally learned how to wash their hands, but that is a subject for another day.

This past weekend, someone said to me, "Marie, you are always so upbeat and so positive. I just don't understand. You're just so positive all the time. You can take the worst situation and turn it into something positive." I was taken aback for a moment because I struggle quite a bit, and I took a second to reflect. Some people will tell you positivity is a choice and while that may be true, I think it's conditioning more than anything.

When we are in the storm, we rely on our conditioning to get us through. I am more positive during stressful situations because I've been training for this for the last five years or so. I have been fortifying my walls by doing personal development and reading books. I have been meditating, a lot. I have been practicing my breathwork, doing yoga, and journaling.

2020 was hard for me too, but I can't imagine how much harder it would have been if I hadn't spent time leading up to it conditioning myself. In the same way, you can't wake up and run a marathon or bench press 200 pounds without training. You cannot take on the weight of the world without proper preparation.

Usain Bolt said he trained four years for a six-second race. Most of us don't spend four minutes training our mental health, let alone four years. While we can't go back and rewrite the way 2020 went down, we can use it as a training tool for the next storm, because there will be another one. It's not if, but when.

That is exactly how life goes, one storm after another. You might get a few months, a year, even several years in between. It is on you to prepare for it right now. Today, we start training for the next storm. What are you going to do so you don't drown? What would have helped you last year? How do you strengthen your spirit to withstand hardships?

A soldier doesn't learn how to use a sword on the battlefield. They learn how to use it during times of peace. They become so skilled with it, it becomes second nature. They can rely on their training when the war finally comes.

What are you going to do the next time you lose somebody close to you and you're battling grief? What are you going to do the next time the economy shits the bed and you're not financially prepared for it? What are you going to do the next time you face heartbreak and the person whom you thought loved you is cheating on you? When it's happening is the worst time to try to figure it out.

The power of hindsight is invaluable during training. You cannot weather a storm you haven't trained for and some of you are drowning in that because you didn't strengthen your muscles ahead of time.

This week I want you to move into training for the next storm by learning from your mistakes, acknowledging your lack of understanding, and discovering how you could be inflaming the situation so that we never put ourselves in a position to suffer the same way again. You will repeat problems until the lesson is learned.

Look for smaller ways to strength train. When we had to put down our sweet boxer boy Diesel, I recognized that this was my children's first taste of grief. I helped them process and understand being sad. I gave them space to cry and supported them through the emotional storm. As a result of this experience, they had tools to help them when my mother-in-law passed the following year.

It wasn't easy, by any means, and losing your pet isn't nearly as bad as losing your grandma. My point is that you learn to swim in the shallow end. Losing our dog was the shallow end of grief, while losing Lynn was the deep end. Protect yourself from drowning by training in the shallow end.

What was the biggest lesson
you learned in 2020?

_____

_____

_____

_____

_____

How can you train for
your next storm?

_____

_____

_____

_____

_____

WEEK 5

90% IS STILL AN A.

One day while a class of elementary kids were learning their multiplication tables, the teacher wrote on the board the following:

9×1=7

9×2=18

9×3=27

She could hear some snickering behind her but kept writing numbers.

9×4=36

9×5=45

9×6=54

9×7=63

The murmuring in the room was growing and she heard one kid whisper "she doesn't even know her multiplication"

9×8=72

9×9=81

9×10=90

When she was done, she looked back at the students and they were all laughing. "What's wrong?" she asked. One boy raised his and said, "You're supposed to be the teacher and you got the easiest one wrong." All the kids giggled. Then the teacher said the following:

"I wrote the first equation wrong on purpose because I wanted you to learn something important...This was for you to know how the world will often treat you. You can see that I wrote the RIGHT thing nine times, but none of you congratulated me for it. Instead, you all laughed and criticized me because of one wrong thing I did. I got 90% correct but now must defend the 10% that was wrong."

The surface lesson is that the world will rarely appreciate the good you do but will more often criticize the one wrong thing. They will hold it against you even when you are 90% good.

As I was thinking about this week's mantra, I was going to leave this one here, but as I have been chewing on this it reminded me of the time I was in yoga teacher training. At the end of the training, we had to perform a practice teach in front of our mentors, which was followed by feedback from each one. Feedback was provided in the form of a "criticism cookie": one constructive criticism sandwiched by two compliments. I had three mentors, which means I received six compliments and three critiques. Eight years have passed, and do you know what still rings in my ears? The three criticisms. In fact, I can't even remember a single compliment.

I was so fixated on the negative, I could not receive the positive. My brain literally did not compute any of the good. I wanted to share this because so many times our brains get conditioned to focus on the negative and it becomes all we can see or think about. We disregard the 90% of good in our lives consumed by the mistakes we've made. Ultimately, we rob ourselves of enjoying the moment.

Another example many of you may relate to is the way we view our bodies. Have you ever found a picture of yourself from the past and thought, wow, *I was sooo skinny back then.* But if you had a time machine and went back into your mind at that time, you didn't think you were skinny. In fact, you likely thought you were fat.

I know I can't be the only one who has done this. Even more pointedly, it wasn't just once; I realized it was a pattern of thinking. I had it happen when I was 25 looking back on 16, when I was 30 looking back on 20, and even more recently, being 40 looking back on 35. For most of my life I have been dissatisfied with my body, always thinking I look fat in clothes and pictures, but then, looking back years later, I realize I was crazy and wish I could be that kind of "fat" again.

Was I ever really fat? Nope! Instead, I now know it was my brain being convinced that my 10% of faults were the whole of me. Because of the mental fixation, I have been the unkindest to myself and it's something I continue to struggle with. Just like you, I am a work in progress and that's okay. I keep gently reminding myself that I deserve grace and that is what I hope for you too.

This week, as you implement the mantra, ask yourself if you are seeing the whole picture or only 10%. Challenge yourself to look at your thoughts from different perspectives. A saying that reinforces this: "Don't let a bad day convince you that you have a bad life." If it starts feeling like you have a bad life, pause and ask yourself: what is good right now? What am I taking for granted? What is working perfectly?

What faults do you hyperfixate on?

_____

_____

_____

_____

_____

How can you redirect those thoughts?

_____

_____

_____

_____

_____

WEEK 6

WHOSE LIFE ARE YOU LIVING?

It's not lost on me that had I been born on the other side of the world, I may not have been allowed to have an education, not allowed to even read, let alone write a book. I might be forced into an arranged marriage. I could be in living in a culture where I would be jailed or killed for my faith. There are parts of this world where people, women more specifically, are suffering because of societal standards.

I wasn't born into those countries. I was born in the good ol' US of A. The land of "freedoms and liberties." Women are allowed to vote, hold jobs, and write books. Most of us are privileged to go to the store and buy Gatorade if we want, or we have an option to pick Powerade if it suits us.

We live in a free nation, but many of us are not free because we are living in a prison in our own minds. We trick ourselves into believing that because we are free to choose, we are free. We disregard the fact that those choices are often dictated by outside influence. The prison of other people's judgment restricts us from finding true freedom.

Every time you make a choice based on someone else's opinion, it was never your choice. Shrinking yourself for other people's comfort, watering yourself down, and playing small doesn't feel like freedom to me, even if you chose to do it. That feels like a cage.

Freedom is doing what you want to do. It's living loud by coloring outside the lines. It is not worrying about what other people think about you. It's a deep knowing that if they don't like me for it, I will be fine. It's the courage to make bold choices. After all, what is the point of freedom if you're not going to use it?

If I put this book out and it flops, it's okay because I did what my heart wanted. I'm not worried if someone doesn't like it or calls it the worst book ever. I know there is a possibility of bad reviews and while I don't like rejection from others, I cannot reject myself and my calling.

What would you do with your life if you weren't concerned with getting your parents' approval? This question can feel particularly challenging if you are a people pleaser. The entire nugget could be making your stomach churn thinking about it. Dream chasing isn't about people-pleasing. It's about remaining faithful to your purpose.

Alignment with that purpose is what fortifies your resolve to keep creating, but we can't achieve alignment if we are constantly compromising what we bring to the table.

This week we focus on honoring our inner wisdom, tapping into our power to create real freedom. One of my favorite sayings that align with this message is: *Stop breaking yourself down into bite-sized pieces, stay whole, and let them choke.* There are no heavier shackles than the weight of other people's opinions.

Whose opinion of you restricts the
choices you make in your life?

_____

_____

_____

_____

_____

How can you break free
from that judgment?

_____

_____

_____

_____

_____

WEEK 7

ALL SHIPS RISE DURING HIGH TIDE.

There once was a farmer known throughout the county for growing excellent-quality wheat. Many other farmers marveled at his crops for being superior grade. Every year the farmer would win prizes in the local and state fairs. Being a dominant force in the wheat industry year after year came with growing acclaim.

One day the local newspaper reached out to do an interview with him. They asked him a bunch of questions about his process. The farmer was an open book, sharing all his secrets, including the fact that he shares his seed with all the neighboring farmers.

The interviewer was puzzled by this fact. "How can you afford to share your seed with your neighbors when they are competing against you in this competition?" The man said, "It's very simple. The wind picks up the pollen from the developing wheat and carries it across from field to field. If my neighbors grow inferior wheat, cross-pollination will steadily degrade the quality of all the wheat, including mine. So it benefits me to help them grow better wheat. If I want to grow the best wheat, I have to help them grow the best wheat."

I believe this story to be one of the most powerful ones I have ever shared. This concept goes in direct opposition to the common thought process in our society. Many people believe that success is in short supply, that because someone else is successful, there's less room for us. Or we think that if we get a little bit of success, we need to guard it at all costs. If we give someone else our secrets, they could come and take what we have earned.

This mindset makes everyone a threat instead of an ally. It also reeks of insecurity. Abundance and success are not in short supply, but there is a shortage for some because of the greed of others. We have forgotten that all ships rise during high tide.

Every year my family hosts a cookoff. Each competitor has to produce a dish onsite using only the resources they brought with them. As a result of living far away, I have not had the opportunity to compete. This year I decided it was finally time to claim my trophy.

In the weeks leading up to the competition, I was in full planning mode. I spent several days testing recipes and techniques to determine which dish would be the best. I decided to make a video series on TikTok sharing all the recipes I was testing. When recounting this to my mom, she warned me that wasn't a smart idea. She insisted it would ruin the element of surprise and give my competitors an advantage by knowing what I was going to cook.

This was another way that scarcity mindset was showing up. I used to subscribe to that fear-based thinking but don't any longer. I knew that I could give them my exact recipe and still win. So while it might take away my element of surprise, it also helps the other cooks elevate their game. We are all bringing our A-game, and no secrets or trickery are needed.

If you are not helping those around you get better, stronger, faster, you aren't showing up as your best self either. Your strategy cannot be based on weakening the competition because as a result, you are weakening yourself. This is the style of thinking I would like you to adopt this week.

Look for people you can build up this week. Choose to operate in confidence by sharing secrets that will help the next in line. By hoarding those ideas and skills, you limit your growth potential, but by sharing you propel everyone to the next level. This open mindset allows for collaboration and celebration within the community. It just feels better when we are all winning.

How can you support your
neighbors this week?

_____

_____

_____

_____

_____

_____

Where does the scarcity
mindset show up in your life?

_____

_____

_____

_____

_____

_____

WEEK 8

WHAT ARE YOU GROWING THROUGH?

Two things we know for sure: change is unavoidable, and time passes whether you like it or not. One thing that is not guaranteed is how much you will grow as a result of the passing of time or changing of seasons. Many of us go through changes several times throughout the year—not only seasons, but we lose friends, switch to different jobs, move homes, and buy new cars, to name a few.

Many changes we have no control over. I can't stop time from ticking, and while I may be able to get Botox, I can't stop the aging process. I can't stop natural disasters or prevent my loved ones from dying. In times like these, it is important to focus on what you DO have control over.

While I may not have a say in some of the changes I will encounter, I do have a choice of whether or not I grow through the changes. First, we must acknowledge that many times we change just for the sake of changing, not for the sake of growing. If you had a job at McDonald's and wanted to get a new job, going to Burger King would be a change, but going to Applebee's would be growth.

Growth is about making a deliberate decision that results in improvement. In 2015 I read a grand total of zero books. I wasn't growing and I knew it. In 2016, I wanted to change that so I read five books. Growth was happening but I wanted to speed it up so in 2017 I read twenty books. I was really impressed with myself, but deep down I knew there was so much more out there for me to learn. In 2018 I read twenty-four books and let me tell you, it was about as hard as you can imagine.

Things came up, I was busy working my three businesses, I have a family, and got sick. Some books were easy to read and others I struggled to get through, but I did it. In a few years, I went from never reading anything other than magazine covers at the grocery store to reading several books a month. This was a conscious choice that eventually led to writing my first book in 2019.

One intentional step sent me on a path that I could have never dreamed of. I had a choice in 2015 of whether or not I was going to get better, stronger, and faster, or if I was going to continue going through the motions. You have to be deliberate in your growth.

Another thing to point out here is that growth doesn't always mean adding. Sometimes growth is about removing. As you grow, you may outgrow the people that have been in your life up to that point. This is normal; not everyone can go where you are going.

I have had to walk away from longtime friendships after realizing that we were no longer morally or ethically aligned. This was a very hard choice to make and left a void in my life. I have never had a lot of friends, so each one is a valued treasure. But the beauty of removing something is that you are creating space for something new.

Although this void hurt my heart, it gave me a chance to get clear on what kind of friendships I needed. I was able to eventually replace those old friendships with new healthy ones. Again, I didn't wait for it, I made a choice that created it.

There are many things you can wing in this life, growth cannot be one of them. What are you going to grow through this week? You can grow any way you want to, but you have to be deliberate. Evaluate the parts of your life that you are unhappy with. What growth needs to happen to change that situation?

I didn't get some of the things I was praying for in my life until I grew into the person who deserved them. Who do you need to become to achieve all the things you want? Start there, and put one foot in front of the other. When the winds of change start blowing this week, hoist your sails and harness them.

What areas in your
life need to grow?

_____

_____

_____

_____

_____

How have you been settling?

_____

_____

_____

_____

_____

WEEK 9

SAVE TO MEMORY.

In the book *You Can't Hurt Me*, David Goggins references a mental cookie jar he uses to hold all his victories. Big and little wins are saved in that jar. So when he's having a really bad day, he can recall all of these small little cookies that he's had to help remind him of what's good in his life and how strong he is.

This resonated with me because I've been doing this my whole life. I just didn't realize it or have the cookie jar analogy to explain it. Not only am I an earth sign, Taurus, but I am obsessed with being in nature. Walking, hiking, or even just sitting in the sand can bring me more joy than diamonds. I scan the skyline at night to look for the moon, take pictures of every sunset, and the moment it starts raining, I am looking for the rainbow.

When I see something really good or when I experience something magical, I say to myself, *save to memory*. It is an intentional decision to put that good memory in my databank for future reference. Why is this so important?

The world is a very dark place, and after 2020 we realized it could feel even darker than we ever imagined. The darkness can feel overwhelming. The cookies or memories become anchors so we don't lose ourselves in the dark.

There is a funny saying: poking around in the dark. When you're looking for something without light, you will end up touching all kinds of things, trying to find what you're looking for. Some of these things are dangerous and could harm you, but you can't tell because you're in the dark. These saved memories become small lights along the way to help you.

If we can start creating this intentional memory-save when good things happen, then we can use them to remind us in the darkness how good life can be.

We must start doing this in our lives sooner rather than later. Even if you're not in a dark place right now, the storm will come. When the storm comes, it's too late to buy flashlights. You have to use the resources you have.

My childhood was filled with darkness. If I hadn't had this inner wisdom as a child, I would likely believe my life was all darkness. I wouldn't remember reenacting "Dirty Dancing" with my cousin Amy, or catching my first fish with my dad before he died, or chasing lightning bugs at my Grandma's house. These moments of sweetness were proof that there was good in the world.

Life is built on duality: light and dark, good and bad, happiness and sadness, yin and yang. One can't exist without the other. As I mentioned, my dad died a few days before my fourth birthday; unfortunately, that means I can count my memories of him on one hand. When I recall those memories I cry, every time.

I'm not crying from grief. I'm crying because those memories are so friggin' special to me. Those memories remind me that I was loved. Even though cancer stole that from me, it can't take away the love. I had that little light and when my stepdad came into my room at night, I would retreat into that love.

Those memories literally saved my life. You have to have memories like that too, the good ones—they are going to save you in the darkness. The key is to train your brain to look for the light in the darkness. It's not easy but is it's like training a muscle—the more you do it, the easier it gets.

Recall some positive memory in your life: a beautiful vacation, the time you got a promotion, maybe the feeling of accomplishment when you graduated college or when you had your first baby. There are plenty of things that have been good in your life. You've just forgotten them.

If you're in a bad space right now, practice looking for something good. I found it in the most random places: turning on really good music and dancing around the house as I'm cleaning, playing games with my kids, and snuggling my dog. These are small things amid the chaos that have helped me get through.

If you're in a good place right now, AWESOME! What parts of this are you saving to memory? There should be plenty of cookies you can collect for future you. It is your job to cultivate a sense of gratitude in those times.

Good times are made sweeter because you have tasted the bad times. This week, focus on filling your cookie jar. Save those good times to memory in anticipation of the darkness, and then don't forget to use it.

Were you able to find five
things you were grateful for this week?

_____

_____

_____

_____

_____

_____

What are some memories you
can use moving forward?

_____

_____

_____

_____

_____

_____

WEEK 10

HAPPINESS SHOULDN'T COST THAT MUCH.

Contrary to popular belief, yoga is not the practice of turning yourself into a pretzel. While we do practice moving our bodies into shapes, this postural part of yoga is only a small portion of what entails the practice. The Yoga Sutras outline eight limbs of the yoga practice and the poses are only one of those limbs. They're not even the first limb.

There are two limbs before we even consider the physical practice, the yamas and niyamas. These two limbs are a set of tenets that teach us how we can navigate life in a spiritually aligned way. Both the yamas and niyamas are broken down into sub-texts, and this week I want to focus on one in particular.

Santosha is the second tenant of the niyamas. It is the practice of contentment, and in my experience, one of the hardest to master. By definition, contentment is a state of satisfaction. This is hard because we live in a capitalistic system in which we're told to always strive and want for more, which means we're never satisfied with what we already have.

We link our happiness to the next promotion, to the size of our house, our salary, our job title, and everything else we are chasing in our lives. These arbitrary finish lines carry our sense of satisfaction with who we are as a person. I'll be good enough when I get my degree. I'll be good enough when I make six figures. I'll be respected in my community when I write a book.

Contentment comes when you can find happiness without all that. True happiness comes from the inside. It cannot be taken away from you. Your worth is not determined by how much money you make, how many degrees you have, what kind of house you live in.

While santosha may be a new term for you, being happy with what you have is not a new or novel idea. Why is it such a hard thing to master? Short answer: consuming feels good. That feeling mimics happiness. When you are sad, buying a new outfit will make you feel happier in that moment. When the feeling fades, you go back for another hit until you're knee-deep in credit card debt and have a closet full of clothes with tags still on them.

We get stuck chasing and forget that *being* is the goal. Santosha is the practice of cultivating a sense of happiness from within, something that can't be taken away because it is not influenced by the external world. The moment you can find your security, your sense of self-worth from inside, you stop attaching it to other things and you free yourself. Freedom equals contentment.

Feeling a compulsion to achieve is detrimental to your health as well. According to www.heartattackfaq.com, more than 805,000 people have a heart attack every year in the United States. While some heart attacks are caused by underlying health disorders, many are caused by lifestyle choices, like eating bad foods, drinking too much, and cigarettes. What is the common denominator here? Consumption. We are consuming these things and the key is to understand why. For many, eating, drinking, and smoking are coping mechanisms of stress, stress induced by the need to achieve. Stress may lead to high blood pressure, which can pose a risk for heart attack and stroke.

That is a big thing for a lot of us. We're on the hamster wheel of chasing the next best thing. It is important to have goals but the price you pay to achieve those goals cannot be your life. It should not cost that much.

As I am putting the finishing touches on this book, the world is watching the Tokyo Olympics. Simone Biles, hands down the GOAT of gymnastics, has removed herself from the competition. She said physically she feels fine but mentally she varies. The amount of pressure she was under to not only perform but carry the team was beyond reasonable expectations.

She made an incredibly tough choice that goes in direct opposition to the American way. She was even quoted as saying, "We hope America still loves us." She knows American love is contingent on performance. So while her death-defying tricks on the mat are noteworthy, the strength she demonstrated in standing up for herself is more remarkable than anyone may realize.

This is the kind of courage we need to cultivate in our own lives. Society will use you up and toss you aside when they are done with you. As you move through your week, I want you to look for where you've attached your happiness to a goal or a possession. What if it never comes? Can you still be happy? If the answer is yes, then you may be starting to understand santosha.

In what areas of your life do you feel obligated to perform?

_____

_____

_____

_____

_____

_____

Can you find peace in your life with what you have now?

_____

_____

_____

_____

_____

WEEK 11

ALL TRAUMA IS CREATED EQUAL.

One thing I didn't know when I started sharing my story was the impact it would have on others. After speaking out publicly, I struggled with being the "poster child" of child sexual abuse. I had to keep it together as complete strangers would approach me to talk about my story. Because I'd shared openly, people often thought my trauma was an open topic for discussion.

I still had a lot of healing to do and one of the things this experience taught me was that I have no right to touch someone's wound. Asking a survivor intimate questions is effectively poking your finger into their wound and we should stop doing that. Instead, I have committed myself to simply listening. I work hard to not pry. How much or little you want to share with me is totally up to you.

How to be a more compassionate listener wasn't the only thing I learned as a result of sharing my story. I am thankful that I am a safe space, but I have noticed a pattern of behavior emerge that I would like to spend some time unpacking. It's something I have determined to be a form of trauma ranking.

In the medical field, the process of trauma ranking is necessary. Health care professionals triage patients to prioritize treatments and address the patients in worse conditions first. Patients with less threatening injuries are moved down the priority list to be treated at a later time. This process CANNOT be applied to the treatment of emotional trauma.

Trauma by definition is a person's emotional response to a distressing experience and there is no scaling system I know of to determine whose emotional reaction is justified and whose isn't based on how badly they were hurt.

You do not have to prop your trauma up next to mine in order to gauge whether or not the feelings you have about it are valid. ALL your feelings are valid and just because someone may have gone through something worse, that doesn't mean you don't have a right to feel what you feel.

Saying things like, I know it's not as bad as what happened to you, or it could have been worse, are forms of gaslighting ourselves into thinking it wasn't as bad as it was. We compare it to other stories that are, in our eyes, worse. That comparison leads us to beat ourselves up for not being stronger. You cannot heal by dismissing or devaluing your experience.

There are no medals for winning the trauma Olympics and I am certainly not interested in playing any games where my feelings are being invalidated because so-and-so had it worse. This is unhealthy and produces no winners.

When I share my story it is not to minimize what you have gone through, but instead to let you know you are not alone. We have both been hurt and we both deserve healing. This week the mantra is short and sweet: All trauma is created equal, including yours!

In what ways do you
invalidate your feelings?

_____

_____

_____

_____

_____

How can you start
honoring your feelings?

_____

_____

_____

_____

_____

WEEK 12

JUDGY MCJUDGERSON

It has been said that annoyances in others' behavior are a reflection of something inside us that needs to be addressed. While recently spending time with a friend who tends to lean into judgment frequently, I found myself irritated. I thought it might be a signal that I, too, had been leaning into judgment. What I determined was that even my annoyances were rooted in my judgment of her judgment.

For the past week I have decided to participate in something I am calling the Judgy McJudgerson Challenge. This was a weeklong deep dive into the conscious and subconscious ways I am judgmental of others. It is something I wanted to self-reflect on because it's really hard to expect the world to do something that you're not willing to acknowledge in yourself.

If you can't do better, you can't ask others to do better. Understanding this, I wanted to look at myself in the mirror and say, how much are you judging other people? As I went through the week, I kept a running list every time I would catch myself being judgmental towards someone.

I'm embarrassed to say I have a lot of room for improvement. As the week progressed I noticed that I was judging on small scales and big scales. Many of my judgments would never be said out loud, but that doesn't mean the thoughts weren't there. I need to look at that and ask, why am I having these thought patterns? Why am I going back towards these negative, petty mindsets? I should know better.

One of the most notable areas of judgment I noticed was with myself. I tend to be hypercritical of everything I do. I am skilled at picking myself apart. There was a direct correlation between how much internal judgment I had going and how much external judgment I cast.

The more I beat myself up, the more I would beat others up too. Sometimes I would cast judgment to feel better about one of my insecurities. I may be bad at this but at least I am not like "that," using the judgment to ease my shame. Other times it would be used to stroke my ego or to feel superior. I used to be like them but I am not anymore. Rounding out the top reasons was pure denial regarding things I needed to address in my own life. It is always easier to point the finger.

Another reason I would move into judgment was that it felt like a form of protection. I would have a story around what other people thought of me, and I would judge them to take away their power to judge me. One problem: it wasn't other people's judgment that was causing this, but my perception of their judgment. There was never any supporting evidence that those people thought the way I imagined they thought.

This entire week has been enlightening and I wanted to share it with you guys for our challenge this week. Where does judgment rear its ugly head in your life? Identify all the times you judge someone for whatever they're doing, their outfit, the way they look, etc. Dissect the areas of your life for deeper insight. Does it occur more at church, with other parents, in your friends' circle? Notice how it shows up in your family dynamic and, more importantly, in your internal critique.

The way we project in the world is a reflection of how we are dialoguing internally. If you are judging everyone else nine times out of ten, it is a way to make you feel better because of the way you're judging yourself. You need somebody to be doing worse than you so you can feel better about what's going on inside.

No one likes looking at the ugly parts of themselves, it was hard to see in me, so I know you may be having some discomfort bubbling around the idea. Remember this journey of growth is not easy; you are supposed to feel uncomfortable. Don't let that stop you from doing it because healing is on the other side.

This week notice all the times you are not giving yourself any grace, all the times that you are judging yourself too harshly for eating the extra cookie or because you didn't get the bed made or you didn't get your Christmas cards out. Whatever it is, stop beating yourself up, and you will naturally stop beating others up too.

How were you
judgmental this week?

_____

_____

_____

_____

_____

_____

Are those judgments linked
to your internal criticism?

_____

_____

_____

_____

_____

_____

WEEK 13

WORRY TREES

One day while driving to work, a man noticed smoke billowing out from under the hood so he pulled over and called a tow truck. After getting his car loaded onto the tow, the man headed into his office. When he got into work he was notified that the company was in financial crisis and as a result, they needed to make layoffs.

His job was intact but because he was the manager, he needed to deliver the bad news to his team. One by one he proceeded to lay off his co-workers, many of whom he had a great relationship with.

Halfway through the day, the mechanic calls to inform him that the repairs on his car were going to cost thousands of dollars and take weeks to complete. This man was having a no-good, downright rotten day. At the end of his workday, one of his colleagues offered to give him a ride home.

They pulled up to his house, his colleague offered to give him a ride the next day and the man expressed his gratitude before getting out of the car. As he walked towards the front porch the man paused next to a huge tree in the yard. He reached his arm out and ran his hand along one of the overhanging branches. After a moment or two, he proceeded into the house.

The next morning his colleague couldn't help but ask about the tree and the man's curious behavior the night before. "Well," the man began, "that is my worry tree. Whenever I have stress from work I hang it on the tree branch so I don't take it in to my family. The funny thing is, sometimes when I come back out in the morning, the worries aren't as heavy."

I love this story because of the symbolic nature of the tree. In my own life, my yoga mat is my worry tree. The place where I hang all my concerns so that for a brief moment I can be free from their weight. I have noticed when I don't set them down before practice I move heavy and sluggish. Conversely, when I do set them down I notice a lightness in my movement. I can breathe easier.

In the same way, the man didn't feel like his burdens were as heavy the next morning, many times I don't feel like my concerns are as bad after a session on my mat. My husband can always tell when I haven't been to yoga. If I am in a particularly foul mood he will ask when I'd last been to yoga.

We both know that yoga makes me a nicer person and when I don't go, my garbage starts to stink up the house. It gives me an outlet to unload my stress so that I don't unload on the people closest to me. It is not their problem that I am stressed and taking it out on them only creates more stress.

I know I advocate for yoga but it is because it changed my life. Maybe it's not your thing and I respect that. If it's not, what is your thing? Where do you go to destress? Do you have a worry tree?

As you move through your week, pay attention to when your stress bubbles up so much it overflows onto the people around you. Notice when your fuse feels shorter than usual or when you lash out at innocent bystanders. No one is exempt from getting frustrated, but that doesn't entitle you to hurt the people you care about simply because you are hurting.

The weight of our lives is a heavy burden, but not one we have to carry all the time. Permit yourself to set it down, even if you can't set it down permanently. Let yourself have a break. The bigger lesson is learning to cultivate emotional intelligence. No one is safe if you turn into the Hulk.

Until you find healthy places to heal, you will keep bleeding on people who didn't cut you. Yoga, art therapy, journaling, and hiking can all be great places to start.

Who do you target your anger
towards when you're stressed?

_____

_____

_____

_____

_____

What are some healthy spaces in your
life where you can destress?

_____

_____

_____

_____

_____

WEEK 14

WHERE YOU START ISN'T WHERE YOU FINISH.

If you know me, then you know food is my love language. I love cooking it just as much as eating it, and one of my favorite things to do is to feed my friends and family. For birthdays and celebrations, I will often make you food instead of buying you a gift. I can put my love into it.

One of my close girlfriends' birthday was coming up so I invited her over for dinner. While she is not a vegan, her husband is, so she doesn't get a lot of meat in her diet. I figured a nice steak dinner with some good wine would be a perfect birthday treat.

I headed off to the local grocery store and picked out a couple of filets and a few other ingredients I needed. There is a liquor store next door and since I only had one bag of groceries, I decided to take it with me instead of going to the car and doubling back. I walked up and down the aisles, looking at the labels, trying to decide what to get.

One bottle is never enough, so I loaded my arms up with three just to be safe and headed to the cashier. I set the grocery bag down on the ground and proceeded to check out. I put my credit card back in my purse as the cashier slid the brown paper bag towards me. Not thinking, I picked up the wine and walked out of the store.

I realized I forgot the steak before I reached my car and turned around. As I was walking in, the woman that was behind me in line was walking out. She politely held the door open for me, and I noticed she carried a grocery store bag.

First, I checked the counter. Nothing. Then I thought maybe I set it down in one of the aisles, so I backtracked my steps. No luck. I was really losing my mind at this point but thought maybe the cashier set it aside. She politely tells me no one turned in any grocery bags and she hadn't seen it.

As I walked out of the liquor store, I realized what had happened. The woman behind me took my bag, then walked right past me with it. That heifer stole my steaks! I fumed as my whole body seethed with anger. Seriously, who the fuck steals someone's food? All I could see is red.

I went back into the grocery store and bought more steaks, and as I swiped my card for another $75, I was practically shaking. This bothered me so much that I was on the verge of tears by the time I started my car. *Take a deep breath, Marie*, I thought, trying to calm down. *At least you could afford to buy more.*

This one thought spun me into a flashback. A memory I had almost forgotten completely came surging in. Having a mother who traded food stamps for drugs meant we very rarely had food in the house. The only meal I would usually get was the free lunch at school. In the summertime that meant I would go sometimes two to three days without eating.

On the verge of starvation, one day I walked down to the local mom & pop store. I knew I didn't have any money and I knew I was too embarrassed to ask for food. I did the next logical thing; I stuffed several Little Debbie brownies down my pants.

It was a small store and the owner had his eye on me the whole time. Before I could get out of the door, he stopped me, made me give back the brownies, and told me never to come back to his store again.

The following week my stepdad pulled into the convenience store and told me to run in and get him a Pepsi. I couldn't tell him I wasn't allowed, and when I tried to walk in the owner stopped me and walked me back out of the store. Seeing this, my stepdad got out of the car and learned of my thievery.

We got home and I walked with dread into the house, knowing whatever came next wasn't going to be good. He told my mom about the incident, adding that I did shit like that because they are too soft on me. Not enough discipline, he yelled, as he draws back his fist and slams it right into my face.

Warm blood streamed down my face and my eyes welled up. A couple of more blows were landed before I was sent to my room without dinner. As I lay in bed, I couldn't tell what hurt more, my empty stomach or my face.

Fast forward back to the present day and all the anger had left my body as I sat in my car weeping uncontrollably. Who steals food? People who are hungry. Granted, that woman was buying alcohol, but I don't know her story. Whatever chain of events led her to make that choice could not have been ideal.

If I had the chance to meet with that woman I would tell her this: I see you because I was you. I know what despair and hopelessness can do to you, but you do not have to accept this life. Being born poor doesn't mean you have to die poor. The same goes for being born into abuse. Whether you are 9, 19, or 49, you can make it. I am proof that you don't have to finish where you start.

This is where I want you to focus our mantra this week. Being a cycle breaker means stopping the pattern for yourself and the next generation. If your circumstances aren't ideal, don't give up. Keep fighting for the life you've been praying for. One day you will wake up and realize you are living it.

What cycles do you need to
break in your life?

_____

_____

_____

_____

_____

_____

What does your ideal
life look like?

_____

_____

_____

_____

_____

_____

WEEK 15

SAFETY NETS

Day 9274 of quarantine. It has been more than "one of those days." Lately it feels like it has been one of those weeks or, more accurately, one of those years. I am riding the struggle bus big time. I haven't showered in four days, I have no desire to get out of these PJs and I know the depleted feeling can backslide into depression if I am not careful.

I can always tell because there is no joy in the things that normally bring me joy—well, maybe the bed, but I wouldn't call it joy as much as an escape. I am just glad you can't smell me right now because you don't deserve to be put through that kind of torture. I'm sliding into this yucky place and I want to share that with you guys.

First, I would feel like a fraud if I pretended everything was rainbows and roses when it isn't. But second, I want to let you know you're not alone if you are feeling like that right now. Sometimes when we do start feeling that way, we start to think that we're alone and that nobody else ever struggles, especially if we're on Facebook and other social media.

Many of you only know me because we met through one of my social media accounts, so I don't want to take away from the good that can happen online. Honestly though, sometimes it feels like the devil's playground for insecurities and self-loathing. It can trick you into thinking that the whole world has sunshine in their pockets, which rubs salt in the wound. It can be hard to tell if anything is real.

This isn't the first time I have felt like this and I know for certain it won't be the last, no matter how many safety mechanisms I put into place. No matter how healthy and good my life becomes, my mental health will always be a work in progress. I have made my peace with that.

This is a battle I will be fighting for the rest of my life. Even the strongest soldiers get weary, so I am not going to beat myself up for being here now. Nobody could predict this pandemic. I couldn't stop the world from going to shit. What I can do is rely on my safety nets.

Since it has been a struggle for so long, I have learned many of my triggers and warning signs. Understanding my patterns allows me to mitigate the spiral faster. I know I need to start reading some personal development. I need to surround myself with people who are in a good place in their lives. I need to get out into nature and ground myself in the dirt with my bare feet. These are all things that I need to do to restore myself to a good, healthy emotional place.

Knowing what to do and doing it are two different things. I have not deployed my nets and I am feeling the effects big time. What happens when you ignore those signals and try to power through? When those bells and whistles start going off and you ignore them, then you spiral and before you know it, you've got mental and emotional pneumonia. That's kind of where I had gotten myself to.

I naively thought I could close my eyes and it would go away. I pridefully thought I was stronger than the storm.

There are many reasons why I have been in a dark place. One of them is that I am an active person. I am go, go, go. People always say to me, Marie, how do you get so much done? Well, it's because I can't sit still. I don't know how to move slowly. I only have two speeds: on and off. I don't have a middle speed, and because we've been in quarantine, I've been sitting around just feeling like I'm withering away.

So today I am going to get myself on a schedule. I need to put myself into a routine because it helps me stay energetically balanced. If I don't,

I'm sitting on the couch eight hours deep into binge-watching "Master-Chef" and feeling like a slob. I haven't been eating right. I've been killing a bottle of wine every single day. No wonder I feel like this.

It's time to deploy the safety net. The work this week is to identify what your safety nets are. What is the combination of your lock? I gave you some examples of what works for me but you need to know what will work for you.

Identify some healthy ways you can be supported the next time your mental health dives. I also want you to remember that the people who love you would be sad to know you are suffering and would certainly be there for you if they knew. They want you to reach out. You are strong enough to get through this and this will pass, too.

What are your triggers?

_____

_____

_____

_____

_____

What are your safety nets?

_____

_____

_____

_____

_____

_____

WEEK 16

EVERYONE LOSES WHEN WINNING IS THE GOAL.

It is November 2020 and our entire country is preparing for what might be the most controversial election in our history. It is, at least, the most brutal one I have ever been a part of. It doesn't matter who you are voting for; everyone is on edge. The world will not be the same after the election and we all know it.

There are valid issues at hand on both sides, but that's not new and I don't think that is what is causing all the distress in our country. We live in a world that glorifies winners and demonizes losers. When your system is set up to make you choose between the right or the left, what you're really doing is picking the team you believe will be a winner.

Everyone wants to be associated with the winner. We have a billion-dollar industry called the NFL that thrives off someone winning and someone losing. Suddenly people who can't even throw a football are screaming at their TVs and having meltdowns in their living rooms because their team didn't win.

We've seen cars flipped in the streets after fans take their celebrations out into the community. Trash cans and businesses are set on fire, and other acts of vandalism are committed, all in the name of victory. A victory that we can take zero credit for because we're not the ones playing the game. Winning is a drug that is poisoning our society and killing our relationships.

We all know someone who has to be right in every situation, and you know that can be hard to deal with if it is your significant other. A healthy relationship cannot be based on one person winning and one person losing. The relationship is sacrificed when we need to dominate our partner.

A system designed to have a winning side and a losing side makes for a zero-sum game. Everyone loses because the goal should be unity. You can't have unity when you are forced to pick a side. It immediately turns the other side into your enemy. An enemy that needs to be defeated.

I don't know either candidate on a personal level. I have not had one-on-one conversations with them, and don't know their true motives. How then can I pledge blind loyalty to either one? I can't, and until I have access to a candidate, I refuse to be played by this us vs. them game.

The bottom line: they are public servants who are paid to make good decisions for the sake of the country. They are not a sports team and the election is not the Super Bowl. Because of that, I will continue to remain skeptical of all politicians. I hope you do too.

Do you know who I do know on a personal level? My neighbor, who voted for the other guy. Do you know who I've had one-on-one conversations with? My family, who doesn't agree with my guy's policy. Do you know whose moral character I know? My friend, who was also forced to pick a side. These people are not my enemies and I am not going to let someone I've never met kill those relationships.

I don't have all the answers for how we are to move forward, but I do know that we need more people focused on solutions and less people focused on winning. That's where conversations can happen, where collaboration occurs, and where ideas are created.

By the time you are reading this, the election has passed and we all know the outcome. This week I would like you to reflect on the relationships you have with people on the other side. If your guy won, did you treat people you love like losers? Did you gloat? How did you conduct yourself because you were on the winning team?

Same thing if you chose the losing party. How did you conduct yourself? Did you have a complete meltdown? Do you like how you were treated? Do you think this is a game worth playing? We have the privilege of hindsight and it's important to use that insight to grow wiser moving forward. We are not playing a game; we are being played.

How does needing to win impact your thinking?

_____

_____

_____

_____

_____

What relationships are you willing to sacrifice for your political leanings?

_____

_____

_____

_____

_____

WEEK 17

YOU'LL RUN OUT OF TIME BEFORE YOU'RE READY.

My 84-year-old father-in-law is the closest thing to a national treasure I can think of. He is a gem of a human being who deserves to be protected at all costs. Recently he came down from Rhode Island for an extended visit. It has filled my heart having him here, creating memories my kids will cherish. Seeing him put my husband in his place has been particularly delightful.

The time I have gotten to spend with him has been invaluable to me as well. Losing my father at such a young age meant I have never had a fatherly figure and I'm grateful for how warmly my father-in-law treats me.

Besides cooking for him, the thing I have enjoyed most is hearing about his life and listening to him retell stories. Not only stories about my troublemaker husband, but what it was like as a black man for the last 84 years. He shares openly about the racism he faced in the '70s when he married a white woman and had biracial children with her.

I know I'm only allowed to be in a biracial relationship with my husband now because his generation made it possible. I have so much respect for them both. Out of curiosity, one day I asked him if he had any regrets and his response still sits with me. "My only regret is that I didn't do more."

He went on to talk about how he wishes he had seen more of the world, tried more things, and did more with his career, but he played it safe. He didn't travel much, partly because he doesn't enjoy flying but also because as a middle-class family with four kids, money for extracurriculars was scarce. It was also partly because he is the most famous man in Newport. Everybody loves Mr. T.

It was a message I didn't even know I needed. I was dragging my feet on starting this book. It was in the "tomorrow pile" until George's message came ringing into my ears at 3 a.m. My mind races at 3 a.m. quite frequently and when that happens, I have learned to not fight it.

When you go to sleep, your subconscious mind goes to work and your conscious mind rests. So what's going on in your life that's causing the unrest, that doesn't allow you to sleep? There are answers here if we can ask the right questions.

On this night it was George's message applied to my life. What will I regret not doing? If I die tomorrow, what would be left undone? What will I have left behind as a legacy? You might think that's pretty morbid, but have you ever stopped to think about your impact on this world? Are you leaving it better than you found it?

I think that a pitfall that many of us face is that we believe we still have time. Other people die young, but we are going to live until we're 100. We compartmentalize our death trajectory in a part of our mind so dark we forget it even exists. So we make plans for tomorrow, we make plans for next week. How many of you have a five-year plan?

You won't believe how many people tell me they want to write a book when I tell them that I have written a book. "One day" they always say, and one day leads to another day, and another. Weeks, months, and years pass with no book.

You are wasting your time and you're going to run out of minutes. There are people who died last night who had dinner plans for today. We're always making plans; the action is where the magic is. I have always known time was limited and I didn't want to waste it, but my father-in-law's message was the reminder I needed and maybe you need the gentle reminder too.

I wrote this book. Now it's your turn.

If you died tomorrow, what would be your biggest regret?

_____

_____

_____

_____

_____

What is stopping you from preventing that regret?

_____

_____

_____

_____

_____

WEEK 18

SIGNS, SIGNS, EVERY-WHERE THERE'S SIGNS.

Warning: Hippy Dippy Yoga Shit coming in hot! Do you ever notice patterns in numbers? For instance, I'll see 11:11 multiple times within a few days or other sequential occurrences that make me stop and say hey, this may not be a coincidence. Then I like to look up what it means to see if there is a message.

Two summers ago I started seeing 444 everywhere: street signs, the clock, my receipt at the convenience store—like I said, everywhere. After looking up the meaning, the number 4 is associated with bad luck in some cultures. For instance, the Chinese and Japanese believe that the number four is associated with death. Buckle up, I thought, it's about to get rough.

After getting a car wash a few days later, I noticed the guy pulling my car around slamming on the brakes aggressively. That didn't seem right, so when my sixteen-year-old son asked to drive home, normally I would say yes, but this time I said no. He asked why and I couldn't tell him a "real" reason. I just knew something wasn't right.

We pulled out of the car wash towards the main intersection with a busy six-lane crossroad. The light ahead was red. I pressed my foot to the brake pedal to start slowing down and it went straight to the floor. I pumped it several more times, banging the pedal on the mat. My heart climbed right into my throat as I realized we were going out into the intersection whether we had a green light or not.

My right arm extended straight out across my son. My car was coasting easily 30 miles per hour at this point, but it felt like it was in slow motion. I was holding my breath, bracing for impact, and right before my car pushed too far into the intersection, my light turned green. We coasted past all six lanes and I pulled into a car shop on the other side. My car pulled to a slow stop right before hitting a car parked in the shop lot.

I got out of the car to inspect what was going on. I could hear liquid, so I dropped down to my knees and looked under the car. Brake fluid was pouring out of my car like a leaky faucet. Apparently, the water pressure from the car wash shot up into a small hole in my undercarriage and severed my brake lines.

I was understandably shaken. Okay, Universe, you've got my attention. 444. I got it. I even went to dinner with one of my girlfriends that night to wine-down. I told her I knew something bad was coming and I was glad I didn't let my son get behind the wheel. Things might not have worked out the way they did.

There are no cheat codes in life, but that doesn't mean there aren't answers and signs all around us if we can learn to look for them. On a physical level, you may notice this more easily. Your body tells you that you are sick long before illness sets in. You may have a runny nose, a tickle in your throat, or some fatigue.

These are all signs from your body. If you listen to those signs you can take some vitamin C and elderberry to boost your immune system or drink some echinacea tea to help fight an oncoming cold. If you don't listen, you could find yourself down for the count.

Sometimes looking for the signs helps you move into corrective action, sometimes it allows you to brace yourself from oncoming storms, and other times it's a gentle reminder that you're on the right path. You can find them in your physical body, out in the world, and in your dreams.

I know some people don't dream, and others don't remember dreams, but I have always had the most vivid dreams. It's so powerful that my entire waking mood could be impacted by it. I have found myself with actual tears running down my face when waking up before and we all know what happens when you dream your partner is cheating on you ... the sheer rage.

In the book *Life Is But A Dream* by Tarak Uday, he reasons that everything in your dreams is a reflection of you. So even if you dream about your spouse, you aren't actually dreaming about your spouse but rather the parts of yourself that your partner represents.

When I dream about my husband cheating, my subconscious mind is sending me a sign, a loud one. My husband represents income stability, achievement, and success. Therefore those dreams are telling me I am not paying as much attention to those areas of my life as I should be. My actions aren't in line with my vows to myself and I am not honoring my goals the way I should.

The work for the week is to actively look for the signs. Consider keeping a dream journal or try remembering dreams from recent weeks. Look for the connections.

Have you ever noticed a link
in patterned numbers?

_____

_____

_____

_____

_____

_____

Can you recall a powerful dream
sending you a sign?

_____

_____

_____

_____

_____

WEEK 19

PROGRESS > PERFECTION.

There was a study done with elite athletes and they were asked one question. If we could give you a drug that would guarantee that you would get a gold Olympic medal but would kill you within five years, would you still take it? More than 50 percent of the elite athletes surveyed said yes, that they would take the drug to get the gold medal even though it would kill them.

Thinking the results were a fluke, they ran the study five more times with other sports. The results were the same. More than 50 percent of elite athletes, top performers in their industry, said that they were willing to die for one perfect performance or to get one gold medal.

While this example is for atheletes, it translates into our everday lives. We would risk it all for perfection rather than settle for being good. Even worse, if we think we can't be perfect at the said task, many won't even try it to begin with. Why do something you can't be the best at?

We suffer from perfection paralysis. I can't tell you how many people have told me they won't try yoga because they can't touch their toes. Like, hello? That is what you learn to do in yoga.

Every master was once a beginner, but if you're not willing the be a beginner, you can never be great. The goal cannot be instant perfection. It has to be progress. I can put my feet behind my head because of all the times I showed up on my mat and I couldn't do it, but I kept trying. There is power in progress.

Listen, I am a recovering perfectionist. I get it. For some, the only time we ever received praise is when we did something excellent. Then a link in your brain is made that you are only loved when you are perfect. Chasing perfect becomes the only goal and everything else feels like a complete failure.

Like the athletes above, pursuing perfection can poison your perspective. What are you sacrificing for this illusion of perfection? For starters, perfectionism has a lot of negative effects on the body. Things like ulcers, constipation, migraines, and even eating disorders can be linked to the desire to be perfect.

Second, it doesn't allow room for the people around you to be imperfect. Grammar Police come to mind. We've all seen the memes or the videos about the difference between your and you're, or their-there-they're. Unless it is your job, correcting someone's grammar in a world of talk-to-text and autocorrect doesn't make you superior. It makes you a dick. I said what I said.

I know I am not the best writer. That doesn't make my message less valuable. Nonetheless, I could feel the insecurity bubbling up while writing this book. I have been having nightmares about commas and question marks because I know there may be people who pick up this book and will tear me to shreds for my poor grammar. If you're one of them, you're probably not ready for most of the messages in this book, no matter how well they're written.

Even though I know my writing is improving, I am anxious about sending this to the editor. I could feel my stomach churning thinking about all the corrections she would make. Each typo or grammatical error is evidence that this book wasn't good. That is her job; I hired her to help me because I know I am far from the best, but in order to create it, I had to release my need to be perfect in my words.

When you give yourself permission to be flawed, you give others permission to be as well. Pay attention to your need to hold others to a higher standard; it could be your perfectionism poisoning your relationship.

Striving for perfection also robs you of your peace. You may never feel satisfied as a result. Even if you did something amazing, you can't enjoy it. You're too busy planning your next conquest or picking apart every small detail.

This week I want you to embrace the power in your progress. Let yourself be a beginner. Try something new. Even if you totally bomb at it, fail flamboyantly, because on the other side of that is growth.

How has perfectionism
impacted your life?

_____

_____

_____

_____

_____

_____

What new things would you
like to try this week?

_____

_____

_____

_____

_____

_____

WEEK 20

TOXIC IS AS TOXIC DOES.

There is a term you may have heard called toxic masculinity. Essentially it is the harmful aspect or shadow side of masculinity. Healthy masculinity allows for a man to tap into his strength, but toxic masculinity says things like "you throw like a girl" or "suck it up, boys don't cry." Toxic masculinity robs our men of their right to have emotions or express weakness.

Another toxicity you may have heard of is toxic positivity. Healthy positivity is based on optimism, the notion that storms don't last forever but toxic positivity is the art of pretending the storm doesn't exist. It is telling someone battling depression to just cheer up or telling someone whose house is on fire to look at the bright side. It is the unwillingness to experience anything other than the good stuff, which often results in the denial, minimization, and invalidation of the authentic human emotional experience.

One more you may not have heard of is toxic forgiveness, you probably haven't heard of it because I am pretty sure I coined the phrase.

Healthy forgiveness is based on not holding grudges, allowing those around you to be imperfect, and it is an incredibly important tool to keeping relationships in a good place.

I even had a chapter in my last book-, Assume No Bad Intent, which basically reminds you that most people aren't intentionally trying to hurt you, so they should be given grace. This kind of forgiveness is found when your husband forgets to take out the trash *again*, or when someone cuts you off while driving.

But I want to look deeper into this toxic ideology around forgiveness when it comes to people that DID intend to hurt you. This one is specific to my fellow survivors of trauma. I struggled for decades trying to forgive the man who tortured me for eight years, and I simply couldn't do it. I would get sad—just forgive him, they would say, and I would get angry. If you just forgave him, this would go away, I was told.

Sprinkle in some poignant cliches like: Forgiveness is an attribute of the strong, forgive others the way Christ forgave his persecutors, or forgive as quickly as you want God to forgive you, and I was more lost than ever. Asking me to forgive the way Christ would have has about the same results as if you asked me to walk on water, raise the dead, or turn water into wine. And if I could tap into any Christ-like superpowers it would be, without question, turning water into wine.

Our society peddles forgiveness as the salve to cure all wounds. It's not. Telling someone to forgive their abuser is not only tone-deaf, but incredibly insensitive to all of the trauma they experienced. Because I couldn't "just forgive" the way everyone told me to, I thought something else was broken in me and it only compounded my shame.

Additionally, it is very important to consider how the idea of forgiveness is weaponized by abusers, cheaters, and manipulators to keep victims in a powerless position. In the same way, a narcissist will gaslight and abusers will say things like, "if you just forgive me I won't do it again," or "you're making this harder because you won't forgive me."

I call bullshit and want to make it perfectly clear that you do NOT have to forgive anyone that intentionally hurt you. I reject any version of strength where forgiveness is held in higher regard than surviving the actual abuse. Period.

Asking someone to forgive their abuser is putting the cart before the horse and an oversimplification of what the process of forgiveness looks like for those who were victims of trauma. We learn to love others by first loving ourselves. How, then, can you ask someone to forgive their tormentor when they haven't learned to forgive themselves?

It all starts inside us, not outside, and most clichés and even scriptures around forgiveness gloss over how hard it is to heal. I'll say it again: You do NOT have to forgive the people who hurt you. Instead, for true healing, I found a few things more beneficial.

First, set up some healthy boundaries. Anyone who has intentionally wounded you needs to be immediately moved out of your life. You cannot heal in the environment that hurt you, and being around that person will continue to reopen the would and make healing so much more complicated, if not impossible.

Next, grieve what you've lost. Your childhood, innocence, ability to trust, physical autonomy, and a healthy self-image are all examples of things stolen from you. Make a list. Ask yourself: how would my life have been if this hadn't happened to me? Then allow yourself to mourn it all and go through the stages as if someone close to you died, BECAUSE THEY DID!

Someone died; it was who you could have been, and we need to acknowledge that. These feelings are hard and people tell you to forgive so they don't have to see you ashamed, angry, or depressed. Trust me, these feelings are normal and denying yourself only stuffs them down even more—and we all know what happens when we keep stuffing it down.

Now that you've grieved, there is some forgiveness needed but this forgiveness is for you. That's right—forgive yourself for all the bad things you did to survive, for all the hard choices you had to make because no one taught you better, for all the coping mechanisms you learned to make it through, for replaying your pain night after night, letting it continue to steal your peace.

Forgive the past you for everything you feel shame for and continue to forgive your future self as you learn to put the pieces back together.

Then begin to take back your power, and tap into your talents. It feels like these things don't exist, but they do—they've just been buried underneath the rubble. Allow yourself to explore new ways of existing that aren't dictated by your damage or, better yet, the antithesis of it.

I felt weak and vulnerable, so I joined the Army with the promise to myself that if anyone ever tried to hurt me again I would be ready. Admittedly this is extreme. You could take some kickboxing classes or self-defense courses to achieve the same effect. I started yoga and it allowed me to get back in touch with my body. Start sharing your story. You are a warrior who danced with the devil and lived to tell the tale. Own your truth.

Over time you will begin to find your footing. You'll start to transition into a place of acceptance regarding the past, the last stage of grief. You will know you're there when things that used to make you cry don't, when thoughts about the past don't elicit a negative response in your body, and when the fear and shame no longer consume your every waking minute. Then, and only then, maybe you can make the final step into forgiveness.

What would your life have
been like without trauma?

_____

_____

_____

_____

_____

Where do you need to implement
healthy boundaries to allow healing?

_____

_____

_____

_____

_____

_____

WEEK 21

A PICTURE SAYS 1,000 WORDS.

Have you ever been on vacation and tried to take a picture of a stunning sunset, or been out at night during a supermoon and wanted to capture its magic? You end up taking 15-20 different angles, trying to get the image to reflect how beautiful the moment is, but the pictures never do justice. Even with a filter and Photoshop, the image you took falls short of showing the true beauty of the moment.

You don't criticize the moon when that happens, or chastise the sunset. You resolve yourself to the fact that the camera isn't capable of capturing the essence. Why don't we apply that same understanding to pictures of ourselves?

We know the camera can't capture the beauty of a sunset, but when we see a picture of ourselves, our first instinct isn't to blame the camera but instead we blame ourselves. Something is wrong with me, we think, and proceed to pick ourselves apart.

Oh God, why am I standing like that, I am so fat, that outfit makes my butt look weird... and on and on. This is a vicious cycle that plays out in the mind so frequently we don't even realize we're doing it most of the time. It is so commonplace and universally accepted among women that we have a set of rules when taking group photos.

First of all, everyone has a good side, and if you're in a photo with your friends it is not out of the ordinary to ask to stand on your good side. Second, whoever is taking the pictures is obligated to take multiple from a variety of different angles with all the phones. Third, and most poignantly, everyone must approve the images before they can be shared.

The "huddle up" as I like to call it, is when the final approval takes place. The group gathers around the phone to review. One person swipes through the images taken and we take a consensus of the best one. What is important to note here is that when someone says that's a good one, the only person they were looking at was themselves.

If Susie says she likes the photo, she only means she likes the way SHE looks in the photo. She didn't notice that Jenny had her eyes closed, or that I had toilet paper on my shoe. The only evaluation she made was whether or not the way she looked was good enough.

When a friend says she doesn't like the photos, we will take more and will also reassure each other that they don't look like a busted can of biscuits. Our friends are crazy for thinking they look bad in the photo when you can see with your own eyes that they look stunning in every photo.

Again we can apply the faulty camera logic to our friends but refuse to accept that the same could be true for ourselves. Maybe, just maybe, the camera can't capture your true beauty either. A picture might say 1,000 words, but chances are they're all made up in your head.

We don't see ourselves the way others do, just like we don't hear ourselves the way others do. I don't know a single person that likes the sound of their own voice. Listening to your playback on voicemail equates to nails on a chalkboard. I think my voice has a toucan-like quality, incredibly squawky with a slight gurgle, as if I have something permanently lodged in my throat.

The look of shock cannot be concealed every time a yoga student tells me how soothing my voice is. I hear it at least once a week and it's unbelievable to me every time. I highly doubt any of those people would intentionally lie to me about my voice, so it is more likely I cannot hear myself without applying a negative inference.

We are not inherently bad or broken. There is nothing wrong with the way we look or the way we sound. If anything, the thing that is broken is our way of thinking about ourselves. The programming is designed to make us not see and hear clearly. That is the only thing that needs to be fixed.

One of the ways I have been working on correcting this thinking pattern is to avoid the huddle. I don't look at the photos. Instead, I tell whoever has the phone they can post any photos they want as long as my eyes are open. That has become the only standard I hold myself to.

Knowing I am predisposed to be critical of myself, I head the thinking off at the pass by not looking. I can't explain how much this has helped me improve my body image and if this nugget resonated with you, maybe you can try it too.

This week I want to remind you that in the same way the camera can't capture the true beauty of a sunset, it cannot capture yours either.

Do you struggle with liking
yourself in photos?

_____

_____

_____

_____

_____

_____

_____

What can you do to prevent going into
negative body-image self-talk?

_____

_____

_____

_____

_____

WEEK 22

HEALING ISN'T A STRAIGHT LINE.

Two months have passed since I touched this book manuscript. The internal deadlines I set for myself have come and gone. Compounding shame with self-loathing, I have been unable to put pen to paper without feeling like a complete fraud. How can I inspire and motivate people when I am drowning in my spiral of depression?

How can I help anyone work through life's challenges if I can't even help myself? With each passing day, the dread continues building, and at least three times I have considered completely scrapping all 50,000 words. With a simple mouse click, it could all be gone. I fantasize about the relief I would feel by not having to complete this book, which morphs into guilt for wanting to abandon my inner calling to help.

Thoughts like: I am not a good writer, I don't know anything about book promotions, this project is destined to fail. Loser, fraud, stupid, you are not that important, get over yourself. Blah blah blah. Nobody cares, Marie. I feel all the terrible things in the world and all I am doing to help is writing a book. It's not enough, I am not enough, why even bother? It's all deepening the descent into my depression and now all I want to do is sleep. Sleep is the only time my brain isn't sad.

Then, on one seemingly insignificant day, the fog begins to lift. I have not done anything remarkable or life-altering to come out of it. The clouds just part in the same way they do after any storm. I am now finally coming out of the funk, and I'm back on the writing wagon. I instantly knew I needed to share this struggle to remain authentic, but also because of our ability to romanticize healing.

The process of healing is one of the messiest and complicated parts of our lives and, all too often, through social media or motivational gurus, we are sold the lie that we are just one book, course, or program away from being whole again. Do books like this and other content created for self-discovery help? Absolutely, but none of them will ever be the fast pass to the front of the healing line, allowing you to skip the ugly parts in the middle.

You might even see someone who has a similar trauma to you that has been doing the work. You admire their growth, make them the poster child of success in your mind. You think, if she can do it so can I, and while that is very true, there are a whole lot of setbacks, meltdowns, and moments of frustration that you weren't privy to, so when you go through setbacks of your own, you can't help but think you are doing something wrong. You're not.

Healing from trauma is very much like navigating grief. It comes in waves. In the beginning, you will feel like you are going to drown, but the more time that passes, the less frequently the waves come crashing in. Sometimes you can go days, weeks, or months without feeling it, and then bam! Out of nowhere, you get the wind knocked out of you.

As time passes you likely read some books, work on your mindset, and put systems in place to help you stay afloat. You may even start to believe you are completely healed. Nothing pushes you off the edge faster than realizing that all your work on yourself cannot stop the next wave from coming. Here is where our mantra for the week comes in.

Healing is not a straight line; it is more like a cha-cha than a march forward. You will have moments of despair and spirals. You will have things come up that you thought you dealt with, only to realize there is still a wound in that place. You will be blindsided by triggers that you didn't even know were triggers. You will feel like you are doing everything right, but something is still very wrong. This is what the journey looks like, and what you are experiencing is the behind-the-scenes work that must be done.

As you process this week's mantra, I want to remind you that it is okay to be a work in progress. There is nothing wrong with you. You are not a failure because you had a setback; you are a warrior because you took a hit and got back up. This journey called life is very much like riding a rollercoaster—the key to surviving is that you don't attach to the highs, and you don't lose yourself in the lows.

How do you define healing?

_____

_____

_____

_____

_____

What areas of your life still need healing?

_____

_____

_____

_____

_____

_____

WEEK 23

WHAT ARE YOU ADDICTED TO?

This week I would like to talk about addiction, but not addiction in the common way we think about it. Drugs, sex, food, gambling, and Candy Crush are the obvious forms of addiction many people struggle with. But I think some people out there are also addicted to their brokenness.

This is a very touchy subject because many times our identity is wrapped up in what has happened to us. There is nothing harder to untangle than our identity and the way we see ourselves. This might not be you, but I'm certain you know someone like this.

They choose bad relationship after bad relationship. You watch the cycle repeat as they ignore all the red flags and fall deeply in love, and before long the relationship turns toxic, there's a huge breakup, and a few weeks later they've met Mr. Next. You ask yourself, why do they keep dating those kinds of people? They know those people are bad for them. Why do they keep going back to those kinds of relationships? It's because that's the only narrative they know.

When you are addicted to your brokenness, you intentionally make choices to keep that narrative going.

It might not be relationships. Maybe they hop from job to job, but not before three months of drama. Or maybe it's the friend who always must one-up you when you have something going on. Everything is an emergency room visit and prayer requests. I am not trying to be insensitive here; I know bad things happen and don't want to dismiss that, but we all know someone who seems to be stuck in a bad place.

All addictions start out as a habit, so if we are going to break the addiction to our brokenness, we must understand the habits of the mind. In 2005, the National Science Foundation published an article regarding research about human thoughts per day. It is estimated that we think upwards of 80,000 thoughts per day and of those thoughts, 95% are repeats from the day prior.

If you have been hurt, especially if it was during your brain's formative years, your trauma plays a big role in how you think and how you see yourself. Those thoughts get repeated in the mind over and over until it becomes a dominant thought process. Now imagine how that engrains itself if you see yourself as a victim.

You are going to start believing that you are a victim, and as with all beliefs you will start looking for evidence, and if you don't find the evidence, you will create it. If you find yourself having a good day and smiling a bit more, it will trigger something inside you. This does not align with your belief system. Victims don't have good days, so you sabotage it.

Another reason habits turn into addictions is because it feels good. Whether it's the high from winning a big hand at the poker table or an having an orgasm, we receive something from the behavior we like. When you're at your most broken is when you get the most attention.

I'll let that one sit for a second.

When you're broken, people show up. They're knocking on your door, checking on you, making sure you're okay, and at that moment, you feel loved and supported. So you consciously, and sometimes subconsciously, recreate those situations to get that feeling as frequently as possible.

That's why people watch horror movies, get into extreme sports like base jumping, or any other crazy stuff like that—it makes you feel alive at that moment. You aren't less alive when you aren't doing those things, but it feels like it. Brokenness feels like that, too, because the emotion is so intense, it cuts right to your heart and you think, I'm bleeding... I must be alive.

You get into the habit of going back to touch the wound because it is a reminder you are alive, but this is not the only way to feel alive. This pattern is destructive, not only for you, but for those around you. There are much healthier ways to remind yourself of this.

This week we need to start intercepting those deeply embedded thought patterns, and redirecting them to more constructive ones. Discover new ways of feeling alive that don't include you feeling like a victim. I'll tell you from my experience, nothing feels better than winning, so maybe this week we move away from being the victim and into being victorious.

Can you identify repeating
stories that activate sadness?

_____

_____

_____

_____

_____

_____

How often do you let
them play?

_____

_____

_____

_____

_____

_____

What would being victorious look like in your life?

_____
_____
_____
_____
_____
_____
_____
_____
_____
_____
_____
_____
_____
_____

WEEK 24

BALLOONS

A middle-school teacher was doing an experiment with their students. They opened a pack of multicolored balloons and handed them out, asking the kids to blow up a balloon and write their name on it. After all the balloons were ready, the teacher collected all of them and threw them into the hallway.

"I want you to go out there and find your balloon," the kids were told. All the kids stampeded out into the hallway. A rainbow of balloons from floor to ceiling erupted. They were squealing and giggling as chaos ensued. Several minutes passed but only one or two of the kids had found their balloon.

The teacher allowed the experiment to go on for a few more minutes. Less than half the class had retrieved their balloon when they were stopped. "Kids, now I want you to restart. Now what I want you to do is to go and find the first balloon that you can see, pick it up and give it to the person it belongs to." The kids file out into the hall and within minutes everyone is lined up with their balloon.

I love this story because it seems that from the time we were born, society has told us to chase balloons. Go out into the world and get a college education, get married, and get a job that has a 401(k) and good PTO. You get told to chase skinny air balloons and then you need to chase bigger-house balloons and nicer-car balloons.

We spend decades of our lives frantically chasing after things beyond our reach. It's no wonder so many of us are feeling unfulfilled and dissatisfied with our lives. In the story, the experiment was only successful when each person helped someone else. I know that in my life, I felt the most fulfilled when I was serving other people, not as a servant but by tapping into my gifts and saying, here is my contribution to making our society better.

Our happiness is not cultivated on the hamster wheel of me, me, me, gimme, gimme more and more. That's why so many lottery winners are broke within a couple of years of winning all that money. Athletes and actors have high drug abuse and suicide rates for this same reason. It's because they were told that if they just got that pro scholarship or if they just got the big movie deal, that they would be happy.

Years of their lives thinking that if they just got the job or if they just got the part or if they just had a certain amount of money, that they would finally be happy. One problem: it's a lie and they're not happy. That is a very painful place to be.

The darkest days I have ever faced were times when I felt like I had no purpose. That my existence was insignificant. My favorite quote that applies to this nugget is from Mahatma Gandhi: "the best way to find yourself is to lose yourself in the service of others." It always reminds me that serving others is the solution.

In sharing this wisdom with friends, a common response I hear is, "but what if you don't know what your purpose or gifts are?" To that, I say, at least we know where to start. Step 1—figure out what lights you up. Start asking a few questions about your talents, hobbies, and passions. Are there organizations you can align with? What is something you can't stop talking about? Are there subjects that you could talk about for hours without getting bored?

This process always reminds me of a scene in "Runaway Bride" with Julia Roberts. In every relationship, she "liked" the same eggs as her partner.

It wasn't until she was single that she could determine which eggs she preferred. She was able to stop conforming and start contributing to her relationships. The same goes for finding yourself in real life.

It's normal to not know your purpose all the time; however, we need to remember that problem is an opportunity, not an obstacle. It's an opportunity to explore yourself on a deeper level. The sooner you begin that process, the better. Although a certain percentage of depression is a chemical imbalance, there is another very significant percentage of depression that is directly related to not serving your purpose in the world, to feeling like your contribution doesn't matter.

As you go through this, remember not to get too hung up on trying to get the most perfect purpose. I used to feel like my purpose needed to be a poetic display of proving my existence mattered. I wrote fourteen versions of my "why". What I thought my purpose was twenty years ago is miles away from my intentions in life now. It's why I think it's dumb to make eighteen-year-olds pick a career major, but I digress.

I feel like the purpose of each day will be different. Some days your purpose will be as simple as being a shoulder to lean on and other days you will inspire someone to make a huge change. Then you'll have days where your only purpose is to survive. All the days are valuable, regardless of how much purpose you think you served.

All of those gifts, talents, and ideas were given to you for a reason. It's time to stop chasing balloons and start chasing what sets our souls on fire, one day at a time.

*What were your favorite
hobbies as a child?*

Can you name three charities that
speak to your heart?

WEEK 25

BLESSINGS IN DISGUISE

Hut → cabin → house → skyscraper.

Horse → carriage →Ford Model T → Tesla with suicide doors.

Bartering → gold → paper money → online banking → crypto.

I've been thinking about the power of progress and innovation. Over time our society has evolved and adapted many times. Every time we go through advancement some people resist the new system. In my family, we call them the old heads—stuck in their ways.

People who are unwilling to adapt from old ways are not realizing the new options are a blessing in disguise. With time, upgrades have made things more convenient, made transportation safer, utilized new technology that has never been seen before. These unwilling-to-adapt people may show up in your life now as the grandparents that can't use texting or email.

Every generation has its version of this resistance. I remember hearing grown folks in the '90s talk about not trusting online banking, how they wanted their money where they could see it, and how ATM cards were the first step to getting microchipped. Now the majority of financial transactions are done online, and I'm still waiting to get chipped.

Today I see it as some of my friends resist new forms of social media. They miss Myspace and Facebook is familiar, therefore they will never be able to create TikTok content or Snap anything. Or there are friends who want to write me a check instead of Venmo. I don't think being "set in your ways" is a helpful mindset. I think that rigid approach to life ends up making things harder than they need to be.

Most of us are creatures of habit and find safety in consistency. We love things to be ritualistic and routine. We love things to be predictable and do them the way they've always been done because it takes a lot less mental investment. This week I want you to think about how this mindset is restricting your life. Think about the times you've said, "we've always done it this way," because that is very closed-off to growth.

We've always done it this way, but that does not mean it's the best way to do it. I saw this meme that said 3+6=9, but so does 5+4 and 2+7. Sometimes we get stuck in our old ways of thinking and we close ourselves off to something new that could change our lives.

About six years ago, I was in a job that I hated. I was driving an hour each way, working 50 hours a week, totally miserable, and I hated every minute of it. I was missing my kid's sporting events and I never had any time for myself. I was stressed to the max and having nightmares about my job.

The problem was that I also had this programming inside of me from my upbringing that you could never walk away from a job until you had another job. Complicating matters even more, this was almost a six-figure income. I could never walk away from that kind of money for something as trivial as being unhappy. I was stuck.

Needing to destress, I found my way to my yoga mat for relief. Yoga always helps me clear my head. This particular class was different. In the middle of the class, the teacher stopped teaching poses and engaged us in a breathing technique designed to let go of things. I knew without question what I needed to let go of. My job.

With every exhale I let go more and more until tears started falling. I wish I could say I had an epiphany and I turned in my letter of resignation the next day, but I was still stuck in my ways of doing it the "right" way. The Universe stepped in, and I was laid off a week to the day after the yoga class.

I should have been upset that I had been laid off, but instead, I was relieved. I realized that losing my job, being laid off was a blessing in disguise because whether you believe in the power of prayer, the law of attraction manifesting, or divine intervention, when you ask for something, the Universe absolutely conspires in your favor. We mustn't restrict that potential by limiting the vehicle it comes it.

Some blessings are obvious, but most blessings don't come with a sign saying, "I am your blessing." It comes dressed as change, transformation, challenges, and suffering. Likely blessings are trying to make their way to you, but can't because it's not coming in the package you've decided it should. Blessings in disguise bring meaning from unexpected places. The trick is to open yourself up to the idea that your blessing may not arrive in the format that you've been asking for.

This week I want you to look for blessings in disguise, something that you weren't looking for, but we find is the definition of serendipity. Challenge old-school ways of thinking because old ways don't open new doors.

In what ways are you being
rigid in your thinking?

_____

_____

_____

_____

_____

_____

Has a bad thing ever turned out to be a
good thing in the long run?

_____

_____

_____

_____

_____

WEEK 26

THE MAHARISHI EFFECT

In the second half of the 1900s, a yogi guru named Maharishi Mahesh Yogi emerged as a leader in transcendental meditation. He had this theory that when people came together and meditated together as a collective whole, their alpha brain waves could radiate out and effect change into their communities.

As a part of the theory, they went out and started doing these scientific studies. They went into twelve major cities known for being war-zone areas and had high violent crime rates. Cities like Jerusalem and Washington, D.C., were included, along with several other large cities throughout the world.

During the studies, they deployed people trained in transcendental meditation with the singular purpose of meditating twice a day, once in the morning and once at night. The purpose was to see what, if anything, would change statistically in those cities. What they found after extensive study and two-plus years of doing this, on the days when they deployed the meditators, violent crime rates in cities like Washington, D.C., decreased by 25 percent. In war-torn cities like Jerusalem, war-related deaths decreased by 80 percent.

The reduction of crime and death was only reflected on the days when the meditation was occurring. On the days when they weren't meditating, the crime rates and the death rates stayed the same. Even more remarkable, the study concluded that it only took 1 percent of a population practicing the mediation technique to produce measurable improvements in the quality of life for the whole population.

Why is this so important? Because it is scientific proof that we can effect change essentially with our brains. With the state of the world, it could feel like you have no power. We think that we can't do anything. I'm only one person. How can I make a change in the world? My vote doesn't matter. My thoughts don't matter. My small act of kindness doesn't matter. Why bother?

What this scientific study proves is that the simple act of meditating can effect change, and it was also reasoned that advanced practitioners could impact the communities at an accelerated rate. For advanced practitioners to have measurable results, it only required 1 percent of the square root of the city's population. So let's do the math for perspective.

The calculator is out because my math skills are not to be trusted. The population of the town I am in is approximately 30,000. The square root of 30,000 is 174. Using Maharishi's calculation you only need one percent of 174 to effect change in this town. One percent equals 1.7 people. We can't have 1.7 people, so we'll round up to two people.

As few as two people meditating in unison can send out enough vibrational effect to change the people around them. So if you think for one second that you don't hold value, that your space doesn't matter, that your actions and thoughts don't matter, you are selling yourself short.

It is reasonable to deduce, based on the Maharishi Effect, that if two people can affect the general population of 30,000, then one person has the power to affect people in your neighborhood, albeit smaller scale. When you're feeling frustrated by your community, feeling like there's nothing that can be done, start with you. Take some time to get yourself in energetic alignment, quiet your mind, send out vibes of peace, meditate on joy and compassion, and allow yourself to radiate those feelings.

Imagine you are a candle and you have a little flame inside of you. As that flame grows, it radiates your whole body. Now you're walking around town like a glowworm. It's going to start transferring onto people in your proximity. It only takes 1 percent; that's all we have to be. We don't have to change the whole world. We just have to change ourselves and become clear about our intention.

The challenge this week will be to carve out five to ten minutes from your day, preferably your morning. Use this time to envision the world you want to live in and then align yourself to that vision, set an intention for the day. In order to be the change, you have to be the 1 percent.

Monday

MEDITATION

INTENTION

REFLECTION

Tuesday

_____

MEDITATION _____

_____

_____

_____

_____

INTENTION _____

_____

_____

_____

REFLECTION _____

_____

_____

_____

Wednesday

MEDITATION

INTENTION

REFLECTION

Thursday

MEDITATION

INTENTION

REFLECTION

Friday

MEDITATION

INTENTION

REFLECTION

Saturday

MEDITATION

INTENTION

REFLECTION

Sunday

_____

MEDITATION _____

_____

_____

_____

_____

INTENTION _____

_____

_____

_____

REFLECTION _____

_____

_____

_____

WEEK 27

PRACTICE THE PAUSE.

There is a big difference between responding and reacting. Now, on the surface level, they kind of sound like the same thing, but they are different. I'll give you an example of why they're not the same. If you're a mom and you have kids, you are going to get this example.

You're busy. You're trying to get the dishes done as the dryer bell dings. You've got a mental checklist going on in your head of what needs to still get done. Your spouse calls to ask about dinner, and the dog just peed on the floor. Right when you think you can't focus on one more thing, your kids run in.

"Mom, mom, mom. Mom, Mom." Their words don't register immediately because you are focused on all the other things, so the only appropriate response for the kids is to get louder. "Mommy, Mom, MOM!" Their words finally pierce through and you don't understand why they're yelling so you snap back, "What!" with a sharp tone.

That is not a response; that's a reaction. It is a reaction because it is emotional. You're aggravated, you're annoyed, and you're frustrated, causing you to react to them instead of responding to them. I would wager that every single one of you does not want to treat your kids that way. They don't deserve your anger at that moment and we certainly don't want our kids to be the place we unload our emotional stress.

You know they're not purposefully trying to be "bad" or intentionally trying to work your nerve. They're just kids doing what kids do. I believe, if you had a clear head in the matter, you would respond more kindly to them. I know there are many times that I can look back at my parenting and I wish I would have responded differently.

Our children are sponges, and if they aren't learning how to emotionally regulate from you, they probably aren't learning it. If you don't want them to respond to you in a nasty way, you can't have a double standard in how you respond to them. They learn from our actions.

I wanted to bring this up because we react more often than we respond. We can't modify behavior until we are aware of it. To quote the classic cartoon G.I. Joe: "Knowing is half the battle." Unless we're willing to identify the areas where we are insufficient or not performing optimally, we can't effect the change that we want.

Another example, for the non-parents reading this book. You're at work and your boss sends a fourth email asking you for the status of a project. You immediately bang out a scathing response that starts with, "Per my last email..." then proceeds to lay into her and read her for filth. Before a beat is missed, your response has popped into her inbox and now you have a strained relationship at work.

My suggestion would be to save that email to drafts, take 15 minutes, and come back to it, reread it, and ask yourself if that's the message you want to communicate because it's angry at first. If you give it some time and sit on it, you might come back and reframe it in a way that's going to be received better. Emotions are temporary.

When we react, we significantly reduce the person we're talking to's ability to receive what we're saying. I would ask you this week to look at how you're reacting versus how you want to respond. Practice the pause. It's a second of space to align your words with whom you want to be.

I understand no one likes repeating themselves and if your frustration is boiling because you have to keep saying the same things, maybe you're not communicating as effectively as you think. Comprehension is the key here, not simply communication. I don't want to just talk for the sake of talking. I want you to understand.

By practicing the pause, it gives me a moment to refine my response and increase its receptivity on the other end. People will never receive your message if they feel like they are being attacked. They're going to get defensive and likely start reacting to you in the same aggressive tone. This will always end in a stalemate.

One of my favorite quotes that align with this week's mantra is from Maya Angelou: "People will forget what you said, people will forget what you do, but people will never forget how you made them feel." As you move through this week, take some time to think about how you want others to feel in your presence, and start practicing a pause to align your actions with that desire.

How do you want your
words to make people feel?

_____

_____

_____

_____

_____

_____

Were you able to practice the
pause this week?

_____

_____

_____

_____

_____

_____

WEEK 28

ANYTHING YOU'RE NOT CHANGING, YOU ARE CHOOSING.

At some point in your life, you're going to have something in your life you're not happy with. Whether it's your physical fitness, diet, finances, relationships, level of education, a job—something will feel like it's lacking.

It is natural and healthy to want to make changes in your life, but talking about it and *being* about it are two totally different things. It is easy to talk about making changes in our lives. It's much harder to put the changes in place.

I practice the three-strikes-you're-out method. If I talk about something more than three times, it is no longer healthy venting; it is now officially complaining. I don't want to be in that low-frequency space, so if I notice I have brought something up three times and not made a change, I stop talking about it.

By implementing this concept, you'll notice right away how many things you talk about that are completely out of your control. Wasting energy complaining about things like the weather, other people's actions, or how long it takes the repairman to fix your car are not the best use of your time. The three-strikes rule helps you keep it in check so it doesn't spiral you into a negative mindset.

If you catch yourself in this pattern of behavior, it's also important to notice who you are doing it with. Are you surrounding yourself with other negative Nellies? We are the company we keep. When true transformation starts to take hold, some of those people might not be able to go with you. Your growth will move you.

This baseline rule also helps us move into action. You'll become aware of many areas where your words don't align with your actions and be able to look deeper at the problem. I've talked about my finances three times, but I haven't done anything to help me save more money. I haven't added a second source of income to help me get out of this debt. I haven't changed my spending habits. Why am I choosing this?

When you say you want to make a change but don't make one, you create a lack of trust in your mind that negatively impacts your confidence. You say you want to get healthy and eat better, but your subconscious brain knows that isn't true. Every Monday when the start date you set comes and goes, it only further confirms that you don't want to make changes. There is no evidence to prove otherwise.

You may find yourself saying things like: If I just had an accountability partner, I would work out more. If I had a friend to walk with me, I would walk every day. If I had somebody to keep me accountable in my business, to message me and check in on me, I would follow through.

It is no one else's job to make your life choices for you. No one is going to come to your house, pull you out of bed at seven o'clock in the morning, and put your sneakers on for you. It is no one else's job to save money for you. It is no one else's job to slap doughnuts out of your hand. It would be a great world if we had that. But that's not the world we live in.

You are a grown-up. Get your own life together, it is no one's job to be your accountability partner. If you're the kind of person who thinks you need an accountability partner, that is nothing more than an excuse you're giving yourself for your failures.

Have you ever heard the phrase, "If they wanted to, they would?" This is often tossed around as dating advice when relationships aren't matched properly in terms of effort. It applies to your relationship with yourself as well. If you wanted to, you would.

This week I want you to pay attention to what you talk about. Implement the three-strikes rule and kickstart yourself into the changes you are talking about. Sometimes the biggest changes come from the smallest steps, but you have to take the step.

What did you complain about this week?

_____

_____

_____

_____

_____

Do you have negative influences in your life?

_____

_____

_____

_____

_____

_____

WEEK 29

SORRY, NOT SORRY.

Recently, I ran a Facebook poll asking my followers what was the hardest thing for people to say. I got a lot of great responses. Some said "I love you" was hard, others said apologizing, some even said saying goodbye was the hardest word. I absolutely agree—most of those things can be hard to say. But there is one phrase that is much harder for us to say.

"I was wrong."

You might think that falls in line with apologizing but it doesn't. You can apologize and not believe you were wrong. People apologize for a variety of reasons: to keep the peace, mend a broken relationship, or to move on from a fight. Apologizing is not an admission of guilt in many circumstances.

For instance, saying "I am sorry you felt that way" is not the same thing as saying "I am sorry I hurt your feelings." Both statements acknowledge the feelings, but only one takes ownership of our role in it. It is why people will apologize for something but not change their behaviors. They don't recognize the link to their actions so they don't change.

Our society judges and punishes us for making bad choices. Imperfections, making a mistake, or a wrong choice could result in being flogged, gagged, and hung up in the streets. Perhaps not that extreme, but you get the point. It's unfortunate because this fear of being wrong creates a denial of our imperfections and limits our ability to grow.

One of the fundamental things we learn in yoga is focused on observing and checking our ego. When we let our ego drive our practice, most times it's going to result in an injury. The ego does not honor or respect our limitations. What we learn on the yoga mat many times translates into other areas of our lives as well.

Just like in yoga, when we let our ego drive, we put ourselves and those around us in a position to be hurt. When that harm occurs, we can recoil into denial or we can do the harder thing of acknowledging and changing our hurtful behavior. Make no mistake—an apology that doesn't recognize your role is an empty apology, and one that doesn't result in a behavior change is manipulation.

There was a time, not too long ago, when the egos of many men believed that women were inferior. Propped up on the Bible and the patriarchy, they didn't even allow women to vote. The male ego restricted women from holding positions of leadership, earning equal pay, making medical decisions for their bodies, and having personal bank accounts.

The ego said women were to be subservient and, as a result, many women were hurt. We have come a long way from how women were treated during my grandmother's era, but there is still a long way to go, and the only way to get there is to remove the shameful stigma around being wrong.

I don't believe that men today should be punished for the actions of their fathers, but if you know the actions are still hurting people and don't do anything to course correct, then you perpetuate the problem and at that point, you become part of the problem. You wouldn't keep driving if you knew you were driving the wrong way. You would make a U-turn, and that is all an authentic apology is. Course correction.

How different would the world be if we celebrated the courage it takes to acknowledge our harmful actions and make restitutions? Would it make a difference in the way we raise our children? I know I respond better to encouragement than I do to shame.

As a mother, I make lots of bad choices and I own that. I don't care what anybody says about my mothering skills, and I refuse to let mom-shaming move me into ego. I know I'm doing my damnedest to raise good children, but that doesn't mean that I'm perfect. I tell them when I mess up and have had to apologize to them after the fact.

Many parents will scoff at the idea of apologizing to their children, but I advocate for it. I have had to humble myself to my children on more than one occasion. It teaches them many things, including that being wrong isn't the end of the world, the power of an apology, and most important, forgiveness.

Likewise, my denial would have taught them different lessons: I can't be trusted, image is more important than integrity, and lack of accountability. That is not what I want my kids to learn from me, and I am certain you wouldn't want them to learn it from you either.

You have the power to make changes in your life, and it all starts with the courage to look at yourself in the mirror and ask yourself: where are you wrong? Growth is in the ability to look at yourself and say, I royally effed that up. I made a bad choice and I'm going to course correct. I shouldn't have taken that job, I shouldn't have married that person. It's time for a U-turn.

It sucks to be wrong. I don't know anyone that likes it, but you know what sucks more? Hurting the people you love because you let your ego take over. Making a bad choice doesn't make you a bad person, but staying in denial does.

Is there anyone in your life to whom you owe an apology?

_____

_____

_____

_____

_____

_____

How can you celebrate course correction?

_____

_____

_____

_____

_____

_____

WEEK 30

SHE IS NOT MY ENEMY.

Fun fact: I was homeschooled for two years during middle and high school because we moved around so much. It was easier than constantly enrolling in new schools. By the time my sophomore year came around, I had convinced my family to let me return to public school. Always being the new kid amplified my social anxiety and I learned, after 13+ times of being the new girl, that flying under the radar was the way to go, so I had a game plan for starting *another* new school.

Three months into the year I had managed to make a few friends, joined the dance team, and even got invited to homecoming. I liked my classes and was catching up on my grades after quickly realizing how far behind homeschooling had put me. As winter break came and went, I was feeling good about school for the first time in my life.

One day, shortly following the holidays, I was sitting in homeroom waiting for the bell when a beautiful ball of energy named Merrick came bursting into the room. I couldn't take my eyes off her. She was a new girl like me, but she wasn't a new girl like me.

She was outgoing and funny, and people seemed to gravitate towards her. She even had a cool name. Merrick was everything I wasn't, so naturally ... I hated her. I'm talking about full-on teenage mean-girl hated her. Who-does-she-think-she-is-eating-her-crackers-like-that hated her.

I could feel my life force being sucked out of my body every time she came to class. I started to dread school. I found myself shutting down, cutting out people who were friends with her, and avoiding any school event she might be at. As you know, high school is a very small world, so avoiding her was not a feasible solution for the long run. I was eventually forced to sit with her in class. My world was shattering, and I couldn't stop it.

The whole first week sitting together all I could think is "Why did she have to come to school here? Ugh!" Dramatic, I know, but I was fifteen, give me a break. There is a good nugget here, I promise.

Anyone who has ever sat next to an extrovert will tell you that talking is what they do best, so it didn't take Merrick long to sweet-talk her way past my defense mechanisms and into my life. She was warm-hearted and accepting, nothing like the big bad monster I thought she was. She had more musical talent in her pinkie than most had in their whole bodies, and before long she became my best friend.

Although post-high school life eventually pulled us apart, as it always does, I never forgot my first taste of being threatened by another woman's shine. She was not my enemy; she was my inspiration. I'm a firm believer that everyone comes into your life to teach you something. That's why Merrick came to my school.

Now that I have the privilege of hindsight, I know all my hateful feelings were because I wanted to be like her. I wanted to be able to hold the attention of the room unapologetically. I wanted to stop being a wallflower. She had the confidence that I was lacking, and her presence shone a light on that insecurity. It felt like a threat but it was a calling.

When I had this epiphany, I realized I needed to go back through all my relationships to see other times when I might have pre-judged a woman or was overly critical of them. Unfortunately, I'm embarrassed to say, this was not the only time I've had to face this lesson. I was an incredibly insecure person and several more women felt like threats to my womanhood. Some had a higher education than me, some made more money, and others had the nerve to be beautiful when I didn't feel beautiful.

If none of these women was my enemy, why were they placed in my path? Kyla came to inspire me to be a better businessperson, Emily inspired me to work on my physical body after having a baby, and Shauna taught me that family are the people you choose.

As you navigate this week I challenge you to look at your relationships. Who threatens you? Who annoys the hell out of you? Who causes uncontrolled eye-rolling when you hear their name?

These are the people to whom you need to pay attention, because anyone who has the power to cause an emotional and physical reaction in you has been sent to you—placed squarely in your path to teach you something. Also, take time to reflect on past relationships. If you keep attracting the same kind of people, then you haven't learned the lesson yet, so look back in your relationships for patterns. There are clues in all these people that will lead you to healthier relationships moving forward.

Have you ever changed your opinion of someone after getting to know them?

_____

_____

_____

_____

_____

Is there anyone in your life that makes you annoyed?

_____

_____

_____

_____

_____

_____

WEEK 31

NOT ALL SUFFERING IS CREATED EQUAL.

I have delivered two humans out of my body and, make no mistakes about it, I am NOT one of those women who love being pregnant. The only part of being pregnant that I liked was the ability to eat whatever I wanted without judgment, and feeling the boys kick in my belly. Other than those two things, it was miserable.

After nine grueling months of hormone imbalance, weight gain, and joint pain, you experience the grand finale of labor and delivery. This "final stretch" (pun intended) can be one of the hardest things your body will ever go through, even with a smooth delivery and drugs.

Something miraculous happens the moment they lay the baby in your arms for the first time: all of that suffering goes away. Not only that, it feels like it was worth it. Hearing the magical sound of a baby's first cry and seeing them healthy is more powerful than any epidural. This moment is so intoxicating you may not even feel any of the post-delivery stitch-up.

I've been thinking about this idea of suffering, because right now, more than ever, it feels like our world is hurting. Nobody likes suffering but in some circumstances, like having a baby, suffering is a necessary step.

The key is to identify which suffering is avoidable and which suffering is necessary.

There are lots of reasons to feel like you're suffering in your life. Not all suffering is bad, and I think most of us are programmed to believe otherwise. Because it is painful, we run from it, we avoid it. We do anything we can to never experience it.

The kind of suffering that should be avoided is the pain associated with going against your gut instinct, not setting healthy boundaries, and resisting change. These kinds of suffering occur when we aren't in alignment and we can certainly reduce the amount of discomfort that comes from these situations.

Some suffering is only there to make the success sweeter. You can appreciate your success because you endured something to achieve it. Your victory song reflects strength and perseverance in the eye of the storm. You can wear it like a badge of honor.

Likewise, other moments of suffering are designed to help you gain a new perspective. This morning I was shocked to see two fresh pieces of bread in the trash can. I asked my son if he dropped it on the floor and he said no. He threw it away because he decided not to pack lunch for camp and buy instead.

Don't get me wrong, I don't wish suffering on my son, but because he has never missed a meal, he doesn't understand the value of the bread. This is what I mean by suffering providing perspective. The world looks different through the eyes of someone who has been through some shit.

I heard someone say, if you're still cute when you're done with your workout, you didn't work out. The pain associated with working out is necessary to build muscle, and the sweat is a sign you're in the zone of fat burn. The great Muhammad Ali said, "I only start counting sit-ups when it starts hurting, because they're the only ones that count."

Suffering is a by-product of the advances we've made in the world. Everything in our lives is designed to make things easier and more convenient. The downside to a world of ease and convenience is that we forget what it is like to be uncomfortable. Then we suffer when our expectations don't align with reality. A world full of convenience creates a society of people who are easily inconvenienced.

It is why "Karens" rage on fast-food employees for not getting their order fast enough. Their expectations aren't being met, and because we have forgotten how to handle discomfort, the result is a full-on meltdown. How many of you would be miserable if your A/C went out for a few days in the middle of the summer? Even though mankind existed for thousands of years without it, we would suffer considerably.

This week, as things bubble up, instead of running, lean in. How is this suffering helping you grow? It won't feel so bad knowing that on the other side you are giving birth to your dreams, to your successes, and to your victories.

Can you differentiate
between good and bad suffering?

_____

_____

_____

_____

_____

_____

How can you reduce bad suffering?

_____

_____

_____

_____

_____

WEEK 32

THE CRACKS ARE HOW THE LIGHT GETS IN.

A while ago I came across the parable of the cracked pot and I wanted to share it with you as part of our nugget this week. In ancient China, an old man lived in a remote part of the village. He had no access to running water, so every day he would walk down to the local watering hole to get his daily supply.

He only had two buckets he could use for water, so he strapped them to the ends of a long branch and would carry them across his shoulders on his trips to the stream. Over time, one of the pots became worn out and eventually cracked. As the man would walk back from getting his daily supply, the water inside the broken pot would leak out. The man would return with only one full pot of water.

This went on for months. Of course, the perfect pot was very proud of its ability to produce a full pot of water but this only made the cracked pot feel worse. Finally, the leaking pot couldn't stand it anymore. "Can't you see I am broken and useless?" the pot said to its owner.

The old man picked that half-empty pot up and turned towards the path leading to the stream. "Did you not notice that one side of the path has flowers and the other does not? I knew you were leaking water and so I planted seeds along your side of the path. Every day we would walk back together and you would water these flowers. For months I have been able to pick the flowers and bring beauty into my home."

The first time I heard this story I cried because I was a broken pot. I had been questioning everything, feeling like my brokenness restricted my ability to do anything good in the world. This story touched me because it was a reminder that beauty can come because of our brokenness, not in spite of it.

In my last book, I shared with you the ancient Japanese tradition of Kintsugi, the art of repairing broken things with gold to make them stronger, more valuable, and more beautiful. While that parallel is still a valuable way to look at the healing process, how much more empowering is it to know that you don't need to be fixed in order to be valuable?

Sometimes in the pursuit of healing, we convince ourselves that being healed means being free of imperfection—a factory reset, if you will. I have learned this is a misguided understanding of healing. We cannot go back to what we were before the trauma.

Healing is not about repairing to our original state, but rather creating something new altogether. I am a cracked pot and I always will be. We all are and that is okay. Most of us have heard of the Phoenix-rising metaphors, about a resilient bird coming out of the fire.

The story of renewal is told as encouragement during the struggle, but did you know that according to the mythology, the Phoenix set itself on fire? I did not know this. Only one Phoenix can exist at a time. When a Phoenix is preparing to die, it makes a nest and sets itself on fire. From that fire, a new Phoenix is born.

This week I'd like you to set fire to the old you, the one you think you need to be, and birth the new. When I realized that my brokenness could serve me, the game changed. I might have cracked from the pain, but that crack let the light in and now I could see into myself in ways I wouldn't have been able to if I had never been broken in the first place.

How does letting go of who you were
supposed to be make you feel?

_____

_____

_____

_____

_____

Are there any parts of your story that
could be converted to be useful?

_____

_____

_____

_____

_____

WEEK 33

WHAT ARE YOU RUNNING FROM?

"Feeling the need to be busy all the time is a trauma response and fear-based distraction from what you'd be forced to acknowledge and feel if you just slowed down."—MAXINE CARTER

B efore moving on, will you please read that again? Hell, write it down and put it somewhere you can see it, because this quote is powerful!

I'm dropping bombs this week, so brace yourself because I'm letting them fly. There are things in your life that you are not addressing and you are not taking care of because you are choosing to be busy instead. I'm too busy to deal with this, you say to yourself, and then to create a distraction, you load up your plate or you choose to do something else.

One of the reasons why we twist and turn our bodies in yoga is to discover how to be in discomfort. Learning how to breathe through it and clear away the swirling thoughts, especially in a hot yoga class, when you're fighting the external elements as well as the internal turmoil. Some classes last as long as ninety minutes; that's a long time to have to sit in it.

Have you ever stopped to wonder if your need to run 100mph is because you're actually trying to run away? When you have emotional baggage like sadness, grief, or trauma, you run rather than being in that discomfort and digging in by asking, why am I feeling this way? We run, we distract ourselves by turning on a movie, we book fifteen playdates for our kids so that we're always on the go and we never have to slow down. You run from the moment your feet hit the ground until the moment you climb in bed at night and you have no time to process what's going on in your mental and emotional body.

Now I do believe in the power of checking out. I can totally relate to needing some mindless reality TV to give your brain a break. But if days and weeks go by and you've still not completed the task you need a break from, that could be a sign of avoidance. Avoidance never serves the greater good.

In case I haven't made it clear, writing this book is very hard. Partially because I am not a good writer, but more so because it requires me to be vulnerable and open. I can't think of anything more uncomfortable than that. Because it is so hard, everything else seems like a better option. Even things I hate doing, like cleaning out under the sink or reorganizing the linen closet, suddenly feel appealing. I know something is seriously wrong with my head when I am actively choosing manual labor.

It's not all our fault. Emotions are considered a weakness in our world and it negatively impacts both men and women. If a woman is emotional she is labeled hysterical, remarks about it being *that time of the month* are commonplace, and we can see it play out in movies like "A League of Their Own" when Tom Hanks famously yells, "There's no crying in baseball!"

The same thing applies to men. Somewhere along the way, our wires got crossed and it was determined that a lack of emotion equaled strength and the results of that have been catastrophic on the mental health of our men. The birth of toxic masculinity is a direct result of our boys not being allowed to feel.

When you exist in a world that demonizes and ridicules you for feeling, the most logical answer seems to be to stop feeling. One problem: that is impossible, because we are humans and asking humans not to have emotions is like asking the stars not to shine. Not gonna happen.

Instead what we've done is tried to turn the radio up so loud that we can't hear them anymore. Now all of those emotions—the fear, anger, resentment, and jealousy—start to fester. Now we're snapping at people who don't deserve to be snapped at. We're resorting to unhealthy coping mechanisms like excessive drinking, self-medicating, or emotionally eating because we're not processing our feelings appropriately.

We have not been taught how to regulate our emotions and it all starts with being able to sit in the discomfort. The challenge isn't going to have you feeling rainbows and roses; on the contrary, it's going to have you feeling everything you're running from. This week, try to stop running from the pain and start sitting in it a little bit.

The more you can sit in it, the more you can unpack it and the less heavily you're walking around with all of those burdens on your heart. You have to be brave enough to slow down and listen.

What feelings are
you running from?

_____

_____

_____

_____

_____

_____

How is this negatively
impacting your mental health?

_____

_____

_____

_____

_____

_____

WEEK 34

HEAD ON A SWIVEL.

As many of you know I spent eight years in the Army Reserves. My husband served active duty and deployed several times to the Middle East. We are an Army family through and through. As a result, we bring a deeper level of preparedness and planning to everything we do. There is a phrase that soldiers say to each other when heading off into battle that I wanted to share with you: keep your head on a swivel.

This is similar to how theatre actors tell other actors to "break a leg"—a supportive reminder, if you will. The idea of having your head on a swivel means you can see the situation from all points of view, because you never know what direction the threat is going to come from. Telling someone to keep their head on a swivel acknowledges the state of readiness necessary for survival.

I wanted to share this phrase with you this week because it goes in direct contrast to the programming many of us have had during our lifetimes. How many times have you been told to keep your head down, and keep pushing forward? When you are in the middle of a battle that is terrible advice. If your head is down how can you see the challenges that are coming at you? You can't.

By the end of 2020, many people have been engulfed in a similar state of readiness. Each month felt like a new enemy emerged—levels 1-12 of

Jumanji. Survival required flexibility, and many people learned how to pivot in ways they never had before. We learned to adapt or die.

Many businesses closed their doors and the businesses that survived had to abandon traditional work practices. Businesses were forced to reconsider letting employees work from home for the first time. There was a chaotic scramble but in the end, a new way of existing emerged.

Companies learned that employees could still be productive without a manager hovering; they could cut overhead costs and become more profitable. People who had been doing things a certain way for the last decade had to learn how to Zoom and use Google meets. The mental health of many employees improved by not having to commute, deal with office politics, or put on a bra.

As of writing this chapter, we are halfway through 2021 and many businesses are having conversations about returning to work. Having the clear hindsight of 2020, I am left scratching my head. Knowing that they are more profitable and many employees are happier, why would they force employees back into cubicles? The only reasoning I can come up with is that they are desperate to get back to "normal."

News flash: there is no normal to go back to. People are awake now. 2020 snapped us out of autopilot and demanded we grow. You can't undo that growth or take back the lessons we learned. Pandora has been released from the box.

My husband loves war movies. I've seen most military movies more than once: "Saving Private Ryan," "Black Hawk Down," "Platoon," etc. I asked him once why he watched these movies on repeat and he said he missed it. I've heard this from other veterans too after coming home from war.

It is hard to imagine missing being shot at, but when you're in that state of readiness, your systems are firing on all cylinders. You are plugged in and very connected to the moment. I think what they miss is the feeling of being radically alive.

There is a similar feeling amongst thrill chasers. Sky diving, parasailing, eco-racing, and even roller coasters tap into that primal instinct of survival. You get a high from feeling alive. The sensations pierce through the numbness of everyday life.

What it boils down to is the difference between consciously being awake and being asleep. Everyone is awake after 2020. Some people will want to go back to sleep because it is familiar and easy. Some people will refuse to go back to sleep because being awake is when you are the most alive. Each of us will have to make a choice.

Change is the only constant, so while we can hope for things to be smoother sailing moving forward, there will be more bumps and bruises heading our way. It is inevitable. One of my favorite quotes that align with this mantra is from Will Smith, and I'm paraphrasing: if you stay ready, you don't have to get ready.

You can't stay ready with your head in the sand. Going back to sleep makes you vulnerable, so this week I hope you choose to keep your head in the game. Stay alert and don't go back on autopilot. Don't let your neck start to stiffen up. I know the old ways of doing things feel comfortable, but you will certainly find yourself blindsided and ill-prepared for the next battle. Keep your head on a swivel.

What is the biggest lesson
2020 taught you?

_____

_____

_____

_____

_____

How can you stay awake in
your day-to-day life?

_____

_____

_____

_____

_____

_____

WEEK 35

CURIOSITY IS COMPLICATED.

Earlier this week I was cooking live for my Foodie Friday series. One of the viewers commented something along the lines of me being talented at so many different things, and how they could never be that talented. This bothered me for several reasons. First, I don't feel exceptionally talented, and second, I believe everyone has the same ability to excel at things. With enough time and patience, everything can be mastered.

The only difference between me and someone wishing to be more like me is a decision to try. That's my secret. I have failed at more things than most people will ever try. It's a tiny bit of courage coupled with a dose of curiosity.

The reason why this may not make sense to some is that curiosity has been conditioned out of us. Sayings like, curiosity killed the cat, or a jack-of-all-trades is a master of none, are often weaponized to deter people from exploring alternative ways of thinking.

In traditional grade-school programs, there is a lot more being taught than ABCs and 123s. A majority of your time in class is spent on conditioning. This feels wrong because school is the place where your mind is supposed to be opened. Instead, you are taught to follow the leader, color inside the lines, not speak unless you raise your hand, walk in a single-file line. Compliant children are praised and rebellious children are punished.

We've been programmed to believe that being good is dependent on staying inside the boundaries. I've always been someone that asks why. I've always been willing to raise my hand and ask hard questions. Curiosity killed the cat, or that's what people say, but I like to say curiosity breaks the chains of control. Not as catchy, but certainly more accurate.

My curiosity isn't limited to tasks and hobbies, either. I enjoy people who are different than me and having conversations that tickle my brain. I have a lot of friends from many different religions, heritages, and countries. It's an eclectic friend base, which I'm grateful for.

One of my friends is an atheist and she recently wrote a post saying that although she doesn't believe in a god, if there was a god, they would likely be a woman because women are the creators of life. I found this to be a fascinating way to think about it. If God created man and woman in their image, it is not a far stretch to think God must have feminine traits too.

While I appreciated her perspective, many people on her comment feed did not agree. She was called a blasphemer and told she was going to hell. The polarity of these two thought processes tickled my brain and the unraveling went something like this...

Blaspheming is a sin and the punishment for sin without repentance is an eternity in hell. But God is the all-powerful master of the universe who created everything. Why would he be concerned about the doubts of a single human? That's seven billion opinions (not counting people who have already died) he has to consider. Doesn't seem like a loving and merciful God would punish someone who questioned him with the same punishment as a rapist or murder. It's not adding up.

I grew up in the church and every time I would have a question that couldn't be answered, instead of being told an answer, I would be told to write Bible verses. I didn't learn more about God. I learned the church didn't have as many answers as it pretends it does. Pay attention to when fear and shame are being weaponized against you. Control is the goal with anyone that is doing that.

I'm not saying my friend is right or wrong, but I am interested in how she got to that conclusion and I am willing to ask why. The same goes for the naysayers in her comments—I just want to understand where they are coming from, so I allow space for my mind to explore both sides. Here is where I landed: if there is a god, then they created me and gifted me this big beautiful brain and I am going to use it. I am going to keep asking questions and keep seeking answers. That is not a sin, as far as I am concerned.

I read *Untamed* by Glennon Doyle, and she said something poetic that I wanted to share. She said that God is like water and religion is like a glass. Everyone is putting God in a glass but the glass is not God. It is beyond our ability to understand but this makes sense to me, how each religion would see God differently.

Pay attention if this is triggering you in any way and causing you to feel defensive, because I'm simply sharing my perspective. Being curious is the whole point of the week. I must acknowledge the two places I have been punished the most for being curious: church and school. Maybe you have noticed that too.

Pulling this all together, particularly if you do believe in God and that we are made in his image, isn't it possible that you have been put into a glass and the glass is limiting your potential? Curiosity is considering the shapes you could make if you weren't focused on trying to remain in the glass, just as water can be ice, snowflakes, vapor, and rain.

Trying new things will range in scariness. I have signed up for pottery classes and photography lessons; these things were new worlds but didn't register too high on the scary scale. I tried out for the local theatre's musical and for the Baltimore Ravens cheer squad, both of which were much scarier and I was rejected by both. Other things I tried were equally scary but had much more success, like becoming a yoga teacher and writing a book.

All these experiences allowed me to take on new shapes. They allowed me to break free from the container that I had been poured into and tap into a greater part of myself, and I want you to have that same inquiry. Don't spend fifty, sixty, or even seventy years of your life thinking the world belongs in this one cup, because it doesn't.

What have you failed at
recently?

_____

_____

_____

_____

_____

_____

In what areas of your life
can you practice curiosity?

_____

_____

_____

_____

_____

WEEK 36

WILL IT MATTER TOMORROW?

One of my brain's favorite pastimes is a fun little game I like to call What's the Worst That Can Happen? This game is usually played at night as I lie awake imagining every worst-case scenario to everything in my life. I've gotten so good at this game, I don't even need an actual problem to apply it to. I'm an expert-level catastrophizer.

Lying in bed I hear a prop plane fly by, and that's all the inspiration I need to start spinning a worst-case scenario of the plane crashing into my house. Which part of the house would be the safest part for it to hit and which kid I would save first? What about the dog? Would my husband sleep through it? How would it feel to lose everything in a freak accident? And before you know it, I've got tears running down my face as imaginary grief takes over.

This doesn't happen only at night, either. What if somebody's sitting in the back seat of my car when I get in it? What if there is a shooter in the grocery store? What if that semi merges into my lane and wrecks into me? The list goes on and on. I am sure some of you can relate to the spiral. Fear-based imagination is like a horror movie of your own life.

The examples I gave you are the normal day-to-day stories. Lately, it feels like I've had a surge in material to use for this game. People are dying from Covid and in the streets, we are locked in the house and watching more media coverage than usual, it is not a good time to be playing this game. My imagination is running wild and I need to get it in check.

I have to get my shit together for my mental health and for my family. I am on high alert all day; my hypervigilance is in overdrive. The first step to getting myself more balanced with these fear-based stories is identifying the source. Not all the thoughts in my head are mine; some of them are coming from outside influences. Let's get some clarity on that.

Sometimes it is you, but many times it is externally driven. Fear is a very valid emotion, but it can be weaponized by people who have an agenda. News outlets, politicians, and preachers all use fear tactics for control. The world is on edge. It feels like gasoline has been poured all over and the news outlets are holding a box of matches. Who is using your natural fears to emotionally manipulate you?

Realizing I have opened the door, I can close it. I told my husband I was suffering emotionally and we agreed to restrict how much news we allow in the home. I also deliberately and expeditiously removed many negative voices on my social media feeds. A corner was turned, but there is still a lot of ground to take back. These were easy fixes, but I am far from cured.

Fear is a poor use of your imagination and I want to stop letting my mind drift off into the abyss. It's not all external, and I recognize much of my pain is self-inflicted. How do I course-correct when I feel myself falling into this vicious cycle?

The first thing I do is determine the source. If it's outside me, I let it go. If it is inside me then I let myself acknowledge the validity of the fear. It is a possibility that a terrible thing can happen. Although the odds are slim, these bad things could happen. So let's pretend they did and I died today. How much of that storytime will have mattered?

We only have a limited amount of time here. Why am I wasting it worrying? None of that will matter once I die. The fear, the anxiety, and the worry will all be gone and I will have wasted my final minutes with things that I couldn't prevent.

Admittedly, thinking you might die today is a bit morbid, so if that doesn't work, try projecting yourself into the future. Try that story on for a minute. Will this still be impacting me a year from today? The answer is almost always a resounding NO. Even more notedly, I likely won't even remember it, just as I don't remember what I was needlessly catastrophizing a year ago.

For your weekly reflection, I want you to pay attention to every time you find yourself playing the worst-case scenario game, and consider if it's worth the minutes that you're giving it because you're not going to get those minutes back. Every minute you give to your fear is a minute you lose doing something that could be bringing you joy.

What fear stories keep
you up at night?

Where are these stories
coming from?

_____

_____

_____

_____

_____

Will any part of this matter
a year from now?

_____

_____

_____

_____

_____

WEEK 37

WHEN NO ONE IS LOOKING.

Have you heard of the shopping cart theory? It is a simple concept centered around our patterned behaviors with our shopping cart. To return a shopping cart is an easy, convenient task and one we all recognize as the correct and appropriate thing to do. To return the shopping cart is objectively right. There is no situation other than dire emergencies in which a person is not able to return their cart; simultaneously, it is not illegal to abandon your shopping cart in the parking lot.

Therefore, the shopping cart represents itself as the apex example of whether a person will do what is right without being forced to do it. No one will punish you, kill you, or take you to jail if you don't return your shopping cart. Likewise, you gain nothing by returning the shopping cart. You must return the shopping cart out of the goodness of your own heart, simply because it's the right thing to do.

The shopping cart theory can determine whether a person is a good or bad member of society. When I first heard about this theory, I instantly rejected it. *Who the hell can tell me whether I'm a good person or not because I do or do not return my shopping cart?* This entire theory triggered me in a way I didn't expect.

As I lay down for the night I started replaying all the times in my life when I didn't return the shopping cart. Sometimes it was raining, other times I was in a hurry. Most times though, I was being lazy and moving out of apathy. I've even gone as far as to stick it through the two concrete blocks so it doesn't hit anyone else's car. That's how extra lazy I am.

I had lots of excuses for why I didn't return my cart. I desperately wanted to find some sound justification for doing this. I even tried telling myself, it's someone's job to collect the carts and if I return in the cart, then that's taking their job away. But deep down inside, I knew that the right action was to return the cart.

When something bothers me so much I can't sleep, I know I need to address it. Do you know why I dismissed it and why I got defensive? Because it was calling me out and nobody likes being called out. In these moments, you can either go into justification and defensive thinking, or you can acknowledge the error and do better moving forward.

Even knowing this, I still temporarily slipped into trying to excuse my bad choices. Denial tried to set in and I thankfully realized I was going to sacrifice my integrity if I kept going down this path. It is okay to make mistakes and once you know better, you do better. Any time after know-ing better isn't a mistake, but a choice.

There are so many areas of your life to which you can apply this lesson. Pay attention when someone says you hurt their feelings or said some-thing offensive. Notice your reactions to criticism at work or when your partner sets a boundary. If you feel a sense of defensiveness, anger, or dismissiveness, chances are you're denying the work. Those negative feelings are guideposts you want to pay attention to. They keep you in alignment.

Once I latch on to an idea, I spend a lot of time examining it. After mak-ing peace with my past self and committing to always returning my cart, I started thinking about where I never see any carts in the parking lot ... Aldi's. They're always returned.

If you've never been to an Aldi's, it's not like most chain grocery stores. You have to bag your own groceries and the store runs on a small staff to keep costs low, meaning they can't afford to have an employee out in the parking lot cleaning up carts. Instead, the carts require a deposit of a quarter to get one, and you get your money back when you return it.

This system is effective because you are incentivized to return the cart and get your quarter back. It's only twenty-five cents, in the grand scheme of things twenty-five cents is nothing. But psychologically there is a reward/consequence attached to leaving your cart and therefore you are more likely to return the cart for a quarter.

This reflects how conditioned we are for rewards and punishments. If you believe that every right action deserves a reward, you begin to ask "What's in it for me" and that moves you into selfish action. You become externally driven rather than internally. This cannot be a sustainable way to exist if you truly want the world to be a better place.

Our society has to be governed by something more than rewards and punishments. We shouldn't need laws to tell us we aren't allowed to steal or to stop hate crimes. We shouldn't need heaven or hell to incentivize us to be good humans. If I have to hold a gun to your head to get you to do the right thing, then the honor in that action becomes null and void.

The moral of the theory is that until we can become a society capable of ethically moving without any reward or any consequences, we are going to continue to repeat these destructive patterns. It's easy to look at other people and say what they are doing wrong and how they could live a better life. It's easy to shine the mirror on your friends and your family and your neighbors about their poor choices. It is so much harder to self-govern and self-reflect, and that's what we need to do more of in our society.

We need to reflect more on our actions and less on the actions of the world. Until we can fix ourselves, we cannot fix anyone else. If each one of us took the time to fix ourselves, collectively the whole world would get better.

How does the shopping cart theory apply to your life?

_____

_____

_____

_____

_____

_____

Can you become more internally motivated?

_____

_____

_____

_____

_____

WEEK 38

THE VALUE OF
A DOLLAR.

We've been doing a lot of back-to-school shopping this week, and my husband was using cash to pay for some supplies. I rarely have cash these days so when the cashier gave me the change, I was marveling at the bills. When you think about it, money is a funny concept. All the different denominations made of the same thing, paper fibers with ink, were probably made at the same facility on the same printing press. Somewhere along the way, our society determined that one piece of paper was worth $100, and one was only worth $10.

I've been thinking about that a lot because it is a made-up system. It's paper and we just assigned value to it. You know it's made up because it's not universal. If you go from country to country, you need a different currency, and depending on the country, the value of the money could be less than our currency. In countries like Canada, they've even got purple and orange bills, versus our standard green bills here in the U.S.

No country has the power to tell another what its money is worth. They can say what it's worth to them, but they can't determine the value of any other country's money nor accept another country's currency for payment. The only people who can determine its value are the country it belongs to.

The same should go for our internal value system. Unfortunately, the same society that determined the dollar was only worth a dollar will try to tell you what you are worth as well. Is it possible that the value system our society is trying to impose on you is also completely made up? I'm gonna go with yes.

Other people will always try to tell you what you're worth, so it's your job to cultivate that sense of worth within. We do that by understanding what we are, what our value system is from inside. It cannot come from external validation. Your sense of self-worth cannot be dictated by the people around you. It cannot be regulated by your body and how much you weigh. It cannot be reflected by how much money you make at your job. It cannot be co-signed by the moms in your mom group.

They will always try, but if your core value is strong enough and fortified within yourself, those people and their opinions will not influence nor impact your sense of worth. I'll give you an example. I have always worked in the service industry. I waited tables the whole time my husband was deployed to Iraq and we barely made ends meet. I worked doubles through 39 weeks of pregnancy too because we were dependent on that income.

When we moved to Maryland, I stopped waiting tables and I got better-paying office jobs, but I never forgot where I came from and how hard service industry employees work. When we go out to eat, I always pre-bus my table and overtip because I remember what it's like to be on the grind. The 2020 pandemic hit the service industry hard so when things opened back up, I wanted to do more.

My husband and I are in a much better place financially and seeing all the suffering we decided to participate in a tip-the-bill challenge, where you essentially tip the bill. A sixty-nine-dollar bill gave our awesome server a sixty-nine-dollar tip. I was so full of gratitude getting to bless her and I thought that was going to be the end of it.

I didn't post about it publicly because it wasn't about me, but when the owner of the restaurant reached out to personally thank me, I realized how meaningful it would be if more people participated. I decided to post about it a private foodie group in county to inspire others to do the same if they could. The post wasn't up an hour before someone on that feed commented, "Well, way to pat yourself on the back. Don't you think you're so full of yourself? You should try to be more humble and be generous in private. If you've got money to throw away, I'll take it."

I did not expect an ovation or pat on the back, but I also didn't expect backlash for trying to do good in the world. This man was trying to assert his value system onto me, and my generosity triggered something in him causing him to negatively lash out. This is a prime example of why you must cultivate a deeper sense of core value within. My favorite saying aligned with this message is: if you give them permission to feed you, you give them permission to starve you.

When you start allowing other people to be the barometer of your value system, they can move that around as much as they decide to based on how you act and how they feel, and any other fluctuating factors. It will always be a moving target if you let other people set the standard. This is your weekly reminder that your worth is not determined by anyone else. It's determined by you and you alone.

In a society that glorifies the busy person and shames the lazy person, we can innately feel bad by not doing things according to other people's standards. If you're sitting on your couch and feel shame or are the kind of person that can't sit still, it might be because somewhere along the line society has told you that you need to be doing *more* to be valuable. Remember that your worth is not determined by how much you do or do not do.

What are your core values?

_____

_____

_____

_____

_____

_____

*How do others influence
your value system?*

_____

_____

_____

_____

_____

_____

WEEK 39

THE ROOTS MAKE THE FRUITS.

Imagine planting two tomato plants. The first plant is going to be put into the ground in a sunny spot, where it can receive lots of water and care. The second plant is going to be put in a dark and muddy spot, where it doesn't receive any sunlight at all and has poor irrigation.

It is probably obvious which plant is going to be healthy and produce and which one isn't. Even with an elementary-level understanding of plants, you can determine that the environment isn't sustainable for the second plant. This is the same ideology we need when it comes to our personal growth as well.

However, frequently we get distracted by treating the leaves and the fruit while never addressing the underlying condition that caused the bad fruit in the first place. We get stuck in the cycle of treating the symptoms rather than the illness. If you have allergies, you'll understand this analogy better. Zyrtec is a medicine, but it is not a cure for allergies. It treats the runny nose and sneezing, but cannot remove the cause of the allergy. It's an effective symptom treater.

Our lives are propped up by a variety of symptom treaters. Wine, food, shopping, and even exercise can be vices to treat underlying emotions and feelings that aren't properly being addressed. I think we can all relate to the struggle of being fit and healthy: weight-loss boot camps, fitness programs, juice cleanses, fad diets, pills, shakes, and supplements all promise to help you lose that weight.

Chances are you might even lose some weight with these systems, the same way Tylenol may temporarily take away the soreness from a sprained ankle. But the Tylenol is a temporary fix and every four to six hours, the pain will come back. This is likewise why many people gain back all, if not more, weight than they initially lost. The weight is a symptom of something else and the key to true healing and health is to figure out what the root is.

I saw a "motivational" video one time that said if you're running, you don't have time to think about being sad and my whole body instantly cringed. Running can be a healthy symptom treater but if you're not careful, it can spiral into toxic avoidance. I wanted to scream at the creator, you cannot keep running from your feelings and that is terrible advice. What happens when you run yourself right into an injury or when your body gets too old to run?

My closet is packed to the brim. I wish I could insert a picture here of how much clothing and shoes I have collected over the years. I find purging my closet to be incredibly painful, so I still have clothes from 2002 and things with tags on them collecting dust. On the surface you may think this is an easy one to solve—just stop shopping—but shopping is the symptom, not the problem.

The root of the problem stems back to being poor and wearing hand-me-downs my whole life. I never had nice clothes growing up and felt like a full closet was a reflection of my success. Now I'm understanding the problem better, and I can acknowledge how I was putting my sense of worth into my closet. Digging even deeper down, it's not that I buy too much; it's that I NEVER give anything away. I was suffering from a case of a scarcity mindset. Afraid that I wouldn't be able to buy more, it physically pained me to give things away.

So I sat in my closet examining my roots and I had a moment of clarity.

I remembered all the times I had received a bag of "new" clothes from a friend or family member. I might have had a little shame around needing hand-me-downs, but what I remember most is how much joy it brought me getting all that new stuff to pick through and try on. Many of the items in my closet hadn't been worn in years, they were not serving me in any way and by selfishly keeping them I wasn't allowing them to bring joy to anyone else either.

I went through my closet item by item, and instead of feeling the pain of losing things, I felt excited thinking about who was going to get these clothes and how much they would love having them. I imagined them going out on a girl's night in the dresses and their first day at a new job in the business wear. I purged three trash bags full that day and haven't regretted anything I have given away since then either. My closet is still very full but the broken part of me that needed those things to feel good has healed.

The roots make the fruits, and it isn't until we can treat the heart of the problem that we find healing. Anything that only provides temporary relief can never be a permanent solution. This week I hope you evaluate where you have been planted. Pay attention to your symptom treaters and how they may or may not be supporting your growth.

What are your preferred symptom treaters?

_____

_____

_____

_____

_____

_____

How is your environment impacting your growth?

_____

_____

_____

_____

_____

_____

WEEK 40

UNLEARNING

I did a big thing this week. I bought an almost-new car, and not just any new car—I bought a Mercedes. That's right, your girl finally made it to the big leagues. I realize things like this make you guys think I've got my shit together, but I do not, and pretending like this purchase didn't cause me some internal turmoil would be misleading, to say the least.

Truth is, I am so incredibly excited, grateful, and overwhelmed by this blessing but it reminds me of a quote from Eminem: I came from humble beginnings, so I'm somewhat uncomfortable with winning. This quote sums up exactly how I feel in moments like this. I am more comfortable being the food-stamps-and-free-lunch kid, so buying this car caused me to spiral.

The dark side you don't get to see on my IG or FB posts is how much of an imposter I felt, sitting behind the wheel. I know I can afford it and I didn't even worry about my credit score like with cars past, but it still feels like I'm playing pretend, test driving it. The shadow side is it's triggered my sense of worth and the dialogue that I've had my whole life about not being good enough, the who-does-she-think-she-is loop.

It had me thinking of all the other amazing things that were supposed to come my way but didn't because I was getting in my way. One of the biggest battles we face in our lives is feeling worthy. What we're capable of achieving is, nine times out of ten, directly stunted and limited because of our belief in ourselves.

When we don't believe we deserve it, we both consciously and subconsciously sabotage ourselves. We procrastinate, blame, make excuses, all to prove ourselves right. "See," you'll say to yourself, "I was right. I'm not good enough."

I've had ideas on top of ideas about ways that I could transform my life, and a lot of times when those ideas come in, I think, *nope, that's too much. That's too big of a dream. You're asking for too much.* Then I dream smaller and much more reasonable. Why does abundance have to be small and reasonable?

Some of my playing small is from bad programming during my childhood years. This conditioning goes back so far, I almost believed I had been an introvert my whole life. I would use being an introvert as justification for not doing more. Then one day I had a memory pop in my mind of getting in trouble at school for talking too much.

I must have been in kindergarten or first grade at the time. I was a Chatty Cathy who was punished for talking too much and I would have to write sentences: fifty, a hundred, a thousand sentences. I will not talk in class, I will not talk in the halls, I will not talk on the bus. I was forced to repeat that so many times it became embedded in my beliefs. Talking is bad and I am bad for talking. This message was reinforced many more times throughout my life.

During basic training, while buffing the floors during our "down time," I was joking around with my fellow soldiers. The one female drill sergeant came over and yelled at me, "You know, all you ever do is talk. Every time I'm here, I hear talk, talk, talk, talk, talk, talk." I managed to make it to the bathroom before the tears of shame flooded my eyes. Twenty years later and that criticism still stings when I think about it.

Both of these experiences are just examples of ways that I was ashamed for being who I was, and conditioned to speak less, be smaller, invisible, if possible. I was convinced that my opinion didn't have worth, and that my words didn't have value. As a result of that programming, I lived decades of my life in my shell. Thinking that I wasn't good enough, that no one cared about what I had to say.

Every time I have struggled with connecting with people and talking with people, it forced me deeper into my shell. I was at my breaking point when I had no close friends besides my husband and finally he pleaded with me to get out of the car and at least try to talk to the other moms at football practice. Something had to change.

I am happy to report that I no longer call myself an introvert, and I've come so far from that person that most of you may not believe I was ever shy or quiet. I wasn't born an introvert. I was conditioned and trained to not talk so much. I was taught that my words didn't matter, and because I believed that they didn't matter, I didn't use them. It wasn't until I un-learned that, that I was able to realize I'm decent at the using-words thing.

If you want to break that pattern of feeling like you're not good enough, feeling like you're not smart enough, having all those doubts and beliefs that are holding you back, start by pinpointing where the seed was planted. Remember the message about the roots. Something happened to you that programmed you to feel that way. But if you learned it, you could unlearn it. That is the goal for the week.

What do you need
to unlearn?

_____

_____

_____

_____

_____

_____

Who benefits from you
playing small?

_____

_____

_____

_____

_____

_____

WEEK 41

NO ONE IS GOING TO SAVE YOU.

One day, while out for a walk on vacation, a man got distracted and ended up falling into an old abandoned well. The well had dried up but he was pretty deep down in it. The man started calling for help.

"Somebody please come help me?" he called. Time passed and his voice started getting raspy from the shouting. He refused to give up, and he kept calling out, sometimes crying, sometimes angry, and sometimes without any hope. Hours passed and thirst started to take hold, the irony of dying of thirst while in a well was not lost on him.

Finally, a therapist walked by and the guy said, "Please, can you help me?" The therapist said, "Yes, I can help you." She pulled out her stopwatch and her notebook, and she sat down next to the well. "So tell me about your life," she said. The guy started sharing about his life, about his parents, his trauma, and all of the hard things that he had been through.

After forty-five minutes, the therapist said, "Well, this has been enlightening but our time is up for today. If you'd like to make an appointment for next week, I can put you on the book." As the therapist walked away, the guy realized that while the talking was helpful, it wasn't the help he needed.

Time passed. He continued calling for help and after another hour or two, a preacher walked by. "Please, help me!" the man cried out in despair. The preacher said, "Yes, my son, I can help you." The preacher got down on his knees, put his hands to his heart, and said a prayer for the man to be rescued. Then he got up and walked away.

"Somebody, please, somebody come get me, somebody come save me." He continued calling out for help. Finally, a doctor walked by. "I can help," the doctor said, "Are you okay? Do you have any injuries? Are you bleeding?" From the bottom of the well, the man listed all of the things that hurt him physically. After a couple of minutes, the doctor wrote something on a piece of paper and dropped it down the well. The man picks up the piece of paper and realizes it's a prescription. Not the life-line he needed.

I love this story because it showcases how often we look for other people to save us from our mess, from our struggles, and we're conditioned to look for a helping hand. This is what I call the Disney princess mindset. If you grew up a Disney kid like me, then you learned from the movies that you needed a prince to come and save you.

The hard truth is, there is no prince. You must pick up your own sword and you have to save yourself. There it is; it is no one else's job to fix you, to save you, to get you out of the problems that most times you got into yourself.

This week, I want to permit you to take back the power in your life because you're sitting around waiting, twiddling your fingers, when instead you could be saving yourself. You are destined to be the hero of your own story if you'd stop giving other people the power to influence your life. You are in charge here. This is your story.

If you've ever been pregnant, then you know that everyone and their brother has advice to give about being pregnant. Everyone, and I mean everyone, will tell you the "right" way, and if you aren't careful, you could find yourself drowning in their advice. Trusting your inner wisdom doesn't come naturally. It has been conditioned out of us. Entire industries are dependent on you not feeling good enough, smart enough, or capable of figuring it out.

We cannot keep looking externally for internal solutions. We need to start looking inside, where all the answers already are. You have been given all the wisdom that you need. It's time to start trusting it.

Fear shouts but the spirit whispers, so you have to get quiet to listen. Even the most well-intentioned teacher, preacher, therapist, or doctor may still give you bad advice because it is wrapped in their own biases and limited experience. That is why it is imperative we create a sense of trust in our intuition. This week we start listening to our inner teacher and stop giving other people power. The only regrets I have in my life are when I listened to other people instead of my gut instinct.

When I analyze the situation, I recognize that my Spidey senses were tingling but I didn't listen. I trusted the wrong people and I found myself in messes that I should have never been in. Start trusting yourself—you are the hero in your story.

It's not anyone else's job to save you. Take note this week of how often you're giving your power away. Pay attention to how often you're letting someone you deem smarter than you or has more experience than you or makes more money than you tell you what to do with your life. No one will have your best interest at heart more than you.

Do you recall a time when you
ignored our gut instinct?

_____

_____

_____

_____

_____

_____

How can you become a better
listener to your intuition?

_____

_____

_____

_____

_____

_____

WEEK 42

YOU HAVE TO EAT YOUR VEGGIES.

Randomly I had this memory of my aunt pop into my mind and it inspired this week's mantra. I was maybe six or seven and was visiting her house for the day. We had been there most of the day, so she was serving us dinner. As the plate was set in front of me, I cringed.

On the plate, she had a big ol' helping of peas and carrots. Yuck! This was a typical country dinner I was used to—you have to have a veggie, a starch, and meat, but why can't it always be green beans or broccoli?

I hate peas and carrots. So I ate the pork chop and potatoes and then spread out the peas and carrots to make it look like less. "You can't go play until you clean your plate," she calls to me from the kitchen. Everyone else was done and I was the only one left at the table.

I am certain if I tried them now, I wouldn't hate them, but the seven-year-old me could not get them down. I looked around for the dog, hoping I could offload some of these veggies to her, but sadly she was also outside with all the kids. After losing more than an hour of playtime sitting at the table pushing peas around my plate, my older cousin came over with some words of wisdom. "You know what I like to do? I like to eat my vegetables first and save the good stuff for last. Because that way you have something to look forward to after you eat your vegetables." I have subconsciously been eating my veggies first ever since.

As we talked about a few weeks ago, the problem is that some pain is good for you, but because we live in a society of convenience and we want everything to be easy, we're constantly looking for the easy button. Trying to get what we want without having to go through the challenges that are required to get it. We're losing time pushing peas around the plate.

We're looking for a workaround. We're looking for a shortcut. We're looking for the easy button. And we're not getting the things we want because, more often than not, our blessings come disguised as suffering. There is some suffering that you need to go through to become the person who deserves the blessing. There is value in doing things you don't want to do, just like there is value in eating your vegetables.

I am not going to sugarcoat it: not only is it going to suck going through it but it's going to change you. It's going to challenge you. It's going to break your heart to walk away from those toxic relationships. You will be tempted to let those people stay in your life because it's easier. You might be able to get away with letting them hang around for a while, but you're only delaying the inevitable. You can't skip eating your vegetables because they're an integral part of living a healthy life.

We can get food delivered to our door with a push of a button. I have access to the entire Internet on a device that is just as big as a deck of cards. We became spoiled, or as my husband likes to say it, we became soft. I know you're thinking we already covered this and you're right, but we need reminders. In the same way, I have to remind my yoga students to breathe in yoga class. Knowing something and applying it is not the same thing.

You can't just Google exercise to get fit, you can't click a button for confidence, and you can't swipe right for strength. These things are found in doing the things you are avoiding. Your life is not supposed to be easy.

Your strength comes from choosing to do the harder thing even when you don't like it, even when it doesn't feel good. And if you can make that connection and understand that everything that's been brought into your life was put there on purpose to teach you how strong you are, to teach you how capable you are, and to show you what you are made of, you can stop running from it. You can stop avoiding it. You can stop saving it for last. You can eat it first. And then enjoy the good stuff that comes after.

What is the biggest lesson you learned in your life and what storm brought it?

_____

_____

_____

_____

_____

Is there an action you've been avoiding but deep down you know you need to change?

_____

_____

_____

_____

WEEK 43

TWO THINGS CAN BE TRUE AT ONCE.

This week I'd like to start with a mental exercise. All I want you to do is visualize a dog. Make sure you don't skimp on the details. What breed and size is it? Does it have any special coloring or spots? Is this imaginary dog male or female? Allow that picture to develop fully in your imagination.

When my eyes are closed, I imagine a dog like my Chewy—a little white fluffy dog, less than ten pounds, full of energy. But maybe you imagined a rottweiler, or a golden doodle, or maybe an Alaskan husky. More than likely, you imagined a dog similar to your childhood pet or the dog you have now, but we'd both technically be correct if we described what a dog looks like.

I have a few more words that I'd like you to bring to your mind's eye. What does "home" look like to you? How about a man—what does a man look like in your mind? Now, a woman—what does she look and act like? How about the rich? What characteristics does a rich person have? What image comes to mind when you think about a poor person? What about a Black person? What do they look like to you? Now imagine a white person. Keep visualizing. What does a Christian look like? What about a Jewish person? Finally, a Muslim—what does a Muslim look like in your mind?

If fifty people read the challenge above, I am certain there would be fifty different examples. Does that mean that I'm wrong because I saw something different than you saw? No. Does it mean that you're wrong because you saw something different than me? No, because more times than not, our truth is relative to our perspective. As Anaïs Nin said, we don't see things as they are; we see them as we are. We see things through our experiences, our education, and our environment.

Two men set out to climb a mountain, and one man started from the east side, and one started from the west side. The east side of the mountain was a sharp climb up and the climber had to have a rock-climbing experience to navigate up the steep incline successfully. Meanwhile, the west side of the mountain had a lot of trees and brush, making it easier to traverse. Although both climbers arrived at the top of the same mountain, when they recount the story of the climb, each man is going to tell the story differently.

Often our ego tells us that we are right and the way we see things is a fact. That is fortified in our minds if we have the experience to back that belief up, or if we surround ourselves with people who have a similar perspective and consume media that only tells one-sided stories. This practice is referred to as confirmation bias. People display this bias when they select the information that supports their views, ignoring contrary information, or when they interpret ambiguous evidence as supporting their existing attitudes.

But how can anything be absolutely true if 7.8 billion people on the planet see the world differently? The only reasonable thinking is that two things can be true at once. I can say it's been raining here in Maryland and you can say it hasn't rained where you live and we'd both be speaking the truth.

It's a common misconception that unity is defined by like-mindedness, and I would argue that true unity is about embracing all the differences more than focusing on our similarities. Trying to seek out people that have the same flashcard image as us to create our community is not helpful. Trying to convince others that your truth is the only truth is not how you build a healthy community either. How can you truly listen to me if your goal is to convince me to agree with you?

That is like saying you have a box of red crayons and I have a box of red crayons, so we should be friends and we should only align with others who have red crayons. What kind of picture are we going to color? A boring monotone red picture. But if I bring my box of blue crayons and our neighbor has a box of yellow crayons, those are going to complement your box of red crayons. What we can then create is much more complex and beautiful.

The key to this week's mantra is to ask yourself what side of the mountain you climbed up. If we can understand that our experiences and beliefs are incomplete, it allows us an opportunity to make space for other people to have the same. Look around at your network of friends and family. Do they all think like you? If everyone you hang out with thinks like you, you are not going to be able to think new thoughts, and that is the opposite of growth.

Where did those images you
saw in your mind come from
and how are they limited?

_____

_____

_____

_____

_____

When was the last time you spent time
with someone from a different country,
faith, race, or socioeconomic class?

_____

_____

_____

_____

_____

WEEK 44

CTRL-ALT-DEL

Cooking is one of the few places I can lose track of time and, even better, I can set my phone down and zone out. By the time I heard my phone buzzing on the counter I had missed four calls, and my husband's phone was now coming to life on the counter next to mine. My stomach catapulted into my throat as I realized my son was calling and that many missed calls from him meant whatever came next wasn't good.

Heat washed over my face as all my worst fears flashed before my eyes. I pressed the accept button and felt my heart pound as I lifted the phone to my ear. "Mom ... Mom ... oh my God, Mom." It was his voice and I instantly let out the breath I was holding. If he was talking, he was alive and didn't die in a horrible car accident.

He just got his license three days ago, and this was only the third time he had taken my car out by himself. I'd been having horrible anxiety over the last 72 hours and my worst fears flirted with coming to life. As the evening unfolded my husband was able to be on-site within minutes. No people were injured, but my sweet Jaguar was totaled. Insert huge sigh of relief here.

Given the stories I had been telling myself, this was the best possible out-come. I even found myself grateful my son got this hard lesson without anything truly devastating happening. Hands down, he will be a much more cautious driver because of this, and I can always replace my car, which I did, without stressing about money for the first time in my life. A bona fide blessing in disguise.

A few weeks later, while standing in the dealership parking lot helping him test-drive his first car, I realized this wasn't just a lesson for my son about driving. The mere idea of him getting behind the wheel on his own again brought back all the same anxiety I had before he had his accident. I stood in the parking lot trying to catch my breath, summoning all my energy to keep myself composed, but before I knew it, I was in a full-blown panic attack.

My husband and son were heading into the dealership office to finalize the paperwork, and there was no way I could go in with them. I could barely breathe, standing there in the open air—a stuffy office with a mask on was going to put me over the edge. I opted to head to the car to sit down and collect myself.

Up until that moment, I had told myself that my previous anxiety was my intuition about the accident. I did believe in my gut instinct but now I was concluding it wasn't my intuition about his accident that was sending me into a downward spiral. He is one of my most valuable treasures and I have spent his whole life protecting him, and the idea of losing him was crippling. Accidents happen all the time, and I know friends who've lost children in car wrecks. All moms can relate and worry about their kids, so why am I feeling it like this?

When a situation starts causing physical pain in my body I've learned to pay more attention. This was coming up again because I didn't get the lesson the first time. I have to repeat the level because I didn't beat the King Koopa (my '80s babies will appreciate the Mario reference). One universal truth: what we don't fix, we are destined to repeat.

As my breath returned and my thinking became clear it occured to me that I was losing my grip because I was losing control. In case you hadn't realized yet, I am a control freak. I was drowning in all the things I had no control over: other drivers, him being young and absent-minded, the weather, random animals, car malfunctions. I could keep going but I think you get the point. I was consumed by the what-ifs, and that is a control freak's kryptonite.

Identifying the root of the emotional breakdown is the beginning of the process I call CTRL-ALT-DEL. The same way you access your operating system on a computer, you can access your operating system in your mind and body when the system is glitching. What programs are running in the background? It is almost always fear, anger, or shame for me.

After identifying which program is controlling me—in this instance it was fear—I can alter my focus. A simple shift to what I can control usually does the trick. Fear thrives in the unknown, so what can I do to regain control? I can help my son equip his car to be safer, I can use a tracking app that notifies me if he is speeding or hard stopping at lights, I can make sure to continue to educate him on driving safety.

The final step is to delete all the crazy story pop-ups in my brain and labeling them as spam. I don't even open them, knowing that whatever made-up scenario that is trying to take over is going to download the virus of fear.

What fear-based
stories do you have?

_____

_____

_____

_____

_____

_____

How can you redirect
those stories?

_____

_____

_____

_____

_____

WEEK 45

THE MINUTES MATTER.

Have you ever been to a Broadway musical? I have been to a few, but none will ever compare to my first show: "Rent." After the anxiety around the fact that a boy invited me to this show as a date, topped by having to spend all night with him AND his parents, I found myself oozing excitement. I had never done anything fancy like this in my life.

First, I had to get permission, which required his family passed the parent test. This included a mandatory phone call interview and exchange of all contact numbers, including the address and location of the venue/restaurant. But it also had to pass the church test. Growing up in a conservative Christian home, there were lots of rules and restrictions around secular entertainment.

Music, movies, and musicals were all heavily regulated in our home; many Disney movies didn't even make the cut. I am certain that if my family had known what this musical was about, I would not only have been prohibited from going, but also expected to repent for allowing the devil to tempt me. When I say I am surprised I was allowed to go, I mean to this day I am still shocked.

I borrowed a stunning black floral dress from a friend because I did not have one nice enough. The dress had to pass the test too. Nothing above the knee, no visible shoulders, and nothing showing boobs. Anything less than a turtleneck had to get approval. Thankfully, the dress and a pair of my Grandma's dress shoes got the final sign-off.

During the show, I sat on the edge of my seat. Everything about it, from the diversity of the characters to the music to the complex concept, spoke to me. Officially obsessed, I immediately ordered the soundtrack on CD and listened to it on repeat for a month straight. My favorite song from the show is "Seasons of Love."

The hook of the song is "525,600 minutes, 525,000 moments so dear. 525,600 minutes—how do you measure, measure a year?" It asks us to reflect on the moments that truly matter and offers perspective on how much time we have. When was the last time you thought about your life in minutes?

I was thinking about this question a lot when I recently read the book *This Is Where It Ends* by Marieke Nijkamp. I was in awe of the author's ability to break down the entire school shooting plotline, one minute at a time. Each chapter spanning only a few minutes goes into incredible depth and detail, producing a complete book that takes you through fifty-four minutes.

Fifty-four minutes does not seem like a very long time—in fact, the only time an hour feels like a long time is when I am on the treadmill. More than likely, your timeline tracks in bigger increments. You may recount holiday to holiday, vacation to vacation, or even Friday to Friday. How many minutes get lost between these mile markers?

If minutes were dollars, would you spend them so carelessly? I know there is a lot of time I have wasted, and why this week's mantra is a reminder we all need. The minutes matter. A minute doesn't lose its value just because it is a small increment of time. Think about it this way: how much would you give to have one more minute with a loved one that has passed? I'd bankrupt myself for one minute with my father.

Looking at it through this lens, where can we improve our connection to the present moment? What bad habits gobble up time? What things are we not starting because we believe we need more time than we have? This is a big one for many of us.

I am not going to work out because I only have twenty minutes. I am not going to create my art because fifteen minutes isn't enough time to do it perfectly. I don't read because it would take too long to read with only having ten minutes a day. Here's the thing: the time is going to pass anyway.

One minute on the treadmill, educating yourself, or pursuing your dreams is better than no minutes. Making the most of each minute is where the magic is! As you spend your week reflecting, pay attention to the time-sucks. Improve the quality of your life by improving the quality of your minutes.

Do you have any black holes/time-sucks in your day?

_____

_____

_____

_____

_____

How can you make better use of your time?

_____

_____

_____

_____

_____

WEEK 46

WRITE BIGGER CHECKS.

As a graduation present to his son, a father decided to give his boy one of the cars that he had in his backyard. The son initially refused the car, stating it was a piece of junk. The dad said, "Well, why don't you take it down to the dealership and see how much they'll give you for it?" So the son took it down to the dealership and the dealer told him the car is pretty beat up, but they could offer him $1,000 for it.

The son reported back to the father that the offer was for more than he anticipated. The dad instructed him to take it down to the local pawnshop for a second estimate. The pawnbroker took one look at the car, told the boy it was worthless, and offered him a check for $100. The son is frustrated because he expected it to be at least as much as the dealership.

After explaining what happened at the pawnshop, his dad asked him to take it for one more estimate. Take it to that car show that they have every weekend down at Denny's, he instructed him. "See what they offer you for it." Not expecting much to come from this third excursion, the son took it to the show the following weekend.

When the son pulled the car into the lot, he noticed everyone was looking at him oddly. He got out of the car as a man walked up to him. "Nice ride," the man said and the boy was confused. This car is a beater, he thought to himself. "Really?" the boy responded. The man explained the car is a collector's item, a limited-edition model that would easily sell for over $10,000.

I love this story, and I wanted to share it for many reasons, mainly due to how impactfully it demonstrates how the world will determine your value. Imagine I hand you a blank check and ask you to fill it in with what you think you are worth. If you don't know, you may start to solicit input from those around you. Depending on who you receive feedback from, you could be convinced your value is far less than it actually is.

People with a poor money mindset, negative self-image, lack of drive, are never going to value your potential. They are the pawnbrokers in your story. Your friends and family who love you and want you to succeed are more like the dealerships in your life; they see some value, but don't have any insight into your true worth because they can't get past your dusty exterior.

In the story, it wasn't until to boy took the car to a collector that he was able to understand its value. He needed to get an expert opinion from someone who knew the inner workings of the vehicle. Who knows your inner workings more than you?

You are a limited-edition, one-of-a-kind human being. There will never be another one of you and as far as I am concerned, that makes you a high value. This week the challenge is to start showing up as the high-value being that you are. Pay attention to the pawnbrokers in your life who are trying to devalue you.

Resist the urge to settle for the middle ground with your friends and family. Hold yourself to the standard at which you expect to be valued. No one can co-sign your vision or proofread your potential without your permission.

The only person in control of your worth is you. This week I want you to start writing bigger checks to yourself. You're a collector's item, baby.

Where do you look for your
worth to be validated?

_____

_____

_____

_____

_____

_____

How are these sources
limiting your potential?

_____

_____

_____

_____

_____

WEEK 47

SHIT HAPPENS

The weather has finally started to warm up and I am here for it. My dog Chewy is happy too, since I don't walk him as much in the winter because I am a big baby about the cold. I usually don't have to walk him far because he is a small dog, so a mile or two max is all we ever need to go. Being a creature of habit, I usually walk him around the same path every time, passing familiar faces and waving at neighbors as we enjoy some sunshine.

On our walk recently, Chewy started doing his pre-poop circle dance, and as I went to grab the bag dispenser, I realized it had fallen off the leash, leaving me bagless. Horror, disbelief, and embarrassment washed over me as I stood there, knowing I was going to be leaving a landmine on this lawn.

No cars in the driveway—*phew, maybe they're at work*—I thought to myself before scanning the windows of their house, imagining someone sitting inside watching. Were there any neighbors out? I scanned the adjacent homes. I didn't see anyone but just to make sure, I made an exaggerated display and loudly proclaimed, "Oh no, Chewy, we're out of bags," making it very obvious I was out of bags and NOT an asshole pet owner.

Regardless, the shame had set in, so as we walked off from the shit show I was completely in my feelings. I am never going to be able to walk this way again, I thought to myself as we headed home. I couldn't stop thinking about it. Later that day it replayed in my head, then popped into my mind the following day as I planned out our new walking pattern that would safely avoid the crime scene.

As we headed out for our walk, Chewy was confused when I made a left instead of a right at the end of our street, but he was happy to pee on some new mailboxes and put up no fight on the new route. About halfway into our walk, I saw something ahead on the sidewalk, and as we got closer, I realized it was a big rottweiler-sized doo-doo pile right in the center of the sidewalk. I wondered if they ran out of bags too, and imagined how embarrassed they were leaving such a huge pile and, even worse, not in the grass but on the main walking path. I would have been mortified, I thought to myself as we move past it.

I noticed as we carried on with our walk that I had an unsettled feeling bubbling inside. It's the new path and change-up to the routine, I tried to rationalize, but still couldn't shake it. As we rounded the corner to our cul-de-sac it hit me—more like punched me in the face—why I was feeling this way. It wasn't the new path. It was the new thinking that had just occurred.

As I am telling this story now, you would think this was the first time I found a pile of poop on my walks. It is not. I've come across many in my dog-walking life. Sadly, this was the first time I considered extending grace to the dog owner. Even worse, I used to hold resentment and contempt for them. Who leaves dog poop on the sidewalk? How disrespectful, don't buy a dog if you aren't going to clean up after them, and so on. I had no idea how this poop got there but it certainly was due to a POS dog owner.

This, ladies and gentlemen, is how I got to this week's mantra. My ego got a swift kick in the ass that day and I found a blind spot in my thinking that was causing me to be less than kind to my neighbors. It is so easy to judge others for problems you've never had, easy to fall into the shoulda, coulda, woulda air of superiority that comes when education and experience aren't aligned.

Growing up in an individualistic country like the U.S. has made it even more of a problem, because frequently it's a country of ME and not a country of WE. If it affects me, it's a problem, and if it doesn't affect me, it's not. Empathy as such can't be taught from a book. It is learned through experience. Empathy allows space for context and grace, which we need more of in a world riddled with judgment and shame.

My husband said something to me once that has stuck with me. Every human being has the capacity to be good and to be bad. We are all just one terrible event away from either being the best or the worst versions of ourselves. I'm working on reminding myself of this when I am backsliding into the judgment of others. They're likely going through something I have never experienced and therefore I don't 100% know how I would act in that situation.

Shit happens to all of us. It doesn't even matter how it got there or what kind of shit it is, but being able to realize our shit helps us extend grace to others.

Can you recall a time when you
made assumptions about a
situation and were wrong?

_____

_____

_____

_____

_____

How do you make less of those
assumptions moving forward?

_____

_____

_____

_____

_____

_____

WEEK 48

IS IT ALL IN YOUR HEAD?

In the late 1700s, an American doctor by the name of Elisha Perkins invented a medical device called the Tractor, a pair of metal rods that were to be used to help patients suffering from inflammation, rheumatism, epilepsy, and chronic pain. Patients were told the metallic device operated similarly to how a lightning rod attracts lightning; this device would attract the pain and disease out of the body. As popularity grew for these devices, the news spread throughout the medical community.

Sales branched out across the pond and a British physician by the name of John Haygarth began to question the legitimacy of this medical device. Results were favorable but the device went against all his medical training. So, he manufactured fake Tractors from wood and began an independent study with five of his patients suffering from rheumatism. He told his patients all the incredible claims others had experienced and ensured them that the rod would help their pain. At the end of his experiment, four out of five patients experienced an improvement in their pain.

Dr. Haygarth expanded his research to include other physicians and patients from different hospitals, and changed up the fake materials to see what would impact the results. Given all the changes in variables, many patients still claimed improvement in their pain levels. All this effort concluded that it wasn't the Tractor that was helping patients, but rather the patient's belief that the Tractor worked that was causing the pain relief. This phenomenon is now referred to as the placebo effect.

The placebo effect has been used in the development of pharmaceuticals for decades and has become the standard for determining how well a drug works. A drug cannot go to market simply because it demonstrates patient improvement, but it also must demonstrate efficacy above and beyond the patients that received the placebo.

I wanted to share this little history lesson with you because I love it when my mystical woo-woo collides with science. I have talked openly with my yoga students about how stress can negatively impact the body. It manifests as headaches, ulcers, insomnia, and tight muscles, just to name a few, but the placebo effect is proof that it works in reverse too.

Your brain is a magnificent machine with the power to help the body heal from many sicknesses we often turn to drugs for—you know, the drugs that may help your condition but also give you diarrhea, vomiting, weight gain, and an erection that could last four hours. All these things will then require more drugs and more side effects. It's a vicious cycle.

Dr. Haygarth called it imagination, but it boils down to the stories we are telling ourselves. The question I keep asking myself is: what would happen if we could harness that power? What if it could be directed by the quality of your thoughts and stories? That is all stress is, really: a negative story that we let loop until our physical symptoms match the internal turmoil.

This is the part of the mantra where I feel compelled to remind you I AM NOT A DOCTOR, and this is not medical advice. If you are suffering from depression, chronic pain, insomnia, or any other medical condition, please consult your doctor. I am sharing this to inspire deeper thoughts and discovery into your own body and the power your stories have over it.

In my last book we talked about our brains operating like a radio dial. Different stations sing different songs: sad country songs, upbeat pop songs, moving love songs. Sometimes we need to switch off a station that isn't putting us in the mood. The same thing goes for your mind; sometimes the stories we tell ourselves make the mood worse.

As you move through your week ahead, pay attention to the stories you tell yourself. Determine whether they are making you sick and if they are, change the story. One of my favorite quotes about the power of the mind is from Henry Ford, and I'm paraphrasing: If you believe you can, you're right; if you believe you can't, you're right. Maybe you just need a little placebo.

How often do you let your
mind spiral into negative stories?

_____

_____

_____

_____

_____

What can you do to prevent the spiral?

_____

_____

_____

_____

_____

WEEK 49

ME, MYSELF, AND I.

As you know from a few weeks ago, I kind of have a numbers thing, so when I started seeing threes pop up all over the place, I knew it was a sign. Three is the number of balance and harmony. Much of our day-to-day lives is navigated by multitudes of threes that we may not even realize.

Your ABCs and 123s are elementary ways you use threes, but there are so many more. Breakfast, lunch, and dinner—three meals a day are considered a balanced diet. The pyramids are shaped like a triangle—three points for structural stability. The holy trinity and let us not forget the three wise men, and Jesus rising from the dead on the third day.

When things like this come up, I try to slow down and get quiet. What is the message of three that I need to tap into? It wasn't long before the lesson came to me and now I can share it with you. There are three versions of who we are. Stay with me because we are going into the matrix.

The three versions are: the past you with all of your mistakes, failures, regrets, and pain; the present you, living life in the here and now; and the future you, whom you are trying to become. I think it's important to distinguish between these identities. Now, understanding that the number three symbolizes harmony and balance, I know that seeing it everywhere either means I am in it or I'm not and need to make some changes. An imbalance means you are either living too much in the pain of past you, or worrying too much about the future.

The past version of you cannot become the dominating force in your life because it is keeping wounds from healing. Every time we think about our past trauma, the body has the same physiological response, so you can feel like you're going through it all over again. We bury ourselves in the shoulda, coulda, wouldas, and cling tightly to old ways of being.

One of the things that help me break out of the past loop is remembering I'm not that person anymore. Those events brought me to where I am, but I am not her. I am not the victim. I am not a vulnerable little kid. Although I can't change anything that has happened, I am a whole different person now.

Similarly, spending too much time on the future version of you isn't helpful either. It can cause overwhelm and anxiety. We catastrophize all the worst-case scenarios and let the what-ifs play out. Planning for the future is important because it allows us to dream, but the reality is we don't have much control over what is to come and most of the future is unknown.

The balance comes from focusing on what you can control, the present-day version of you. Looking back can't change what has happened, and looking forward can't stop what is to come. It is something we work on every time we step on the yoga mat. At the end of class, we have something called savasana. This is a quiet few minutes at the end of class to help you recharge the body and let the mind rest. One problem: the mind resists quiet. Savasana, for most, is the hardest of all the poses, even though all you're doing is lying down.

The practice, then, is to notice the habits of your mind when it is left to its own devices. Do you go back to past versions of you, replaying the bad, maybe fantasizing about what you should have said to that smart-ass co-worker? Or maybe your mind prefers to lean into the future, filling the quiet space with checklists, chores, and planning?

I am not in any way saying we shouldn't look back or forward. What I hope for you this week is that you work instead on becoming more balanced. Think of it like a teeter-totter (or see-saw, depending on where you're from). If one side is too heavy, the ride is no fun for anyone, but it is most fun when it is balanced.

The goal this week is to learn to tap into the past and the future but not plant there. Be in the moment where all of your life is happening in real time. Take back your minutes by being more present in the moment.

How did you practice
presence this week?

_____

_____

_____

_____

_____

Was it harder or easier than you
anticipated?

_____

_____

_____

_____

_____

_____

WEEK 50

WRING IT OUT.

I'm guessing we all know what an energy vampire is, right? I can give you an overview of it in case you're not familiar with that term. An energy vampire is someone who sucks the life out of you. Any time they show up, you can feel them draining you. They're narcissists, the drama queens, or the people who are always unloading their problems on you.

They consume all the energy in the room because they're incredibly selfish. We all know people like that; someone specific probably popped into your mind while reading this paragraph. I can name at least three or four people like that whom I know in my life right now. Even with all my barriers, even with all my healthy boundaries, they still make their way in.

Most of us have likely started to identify those kinds of people in our lives already. You keep them at a distance, only engaging in small doses. Protecting yourself before you're going to spend time with them so that your energy is going to be preserved is key. The thing about energy vampires is that they need to feed, and their prey of choice is the empaths, the fixers, the healers, and the givers. If you fall into one of those categories then this mantra is for you.

I don't want to spend any more time talking about the energy vampires; they take enough because they are suckers. What you might not realize, though, is that if you are an empath, teacher, energy worker, or healer, you are an absorber. The analogy that I've been using this week to describe these people is that they are very much like a sponge. As you go through your day, from the time you wake up until the time you close your eyes at the end of the night, you are absorbing other people's energy, not on purpose, not selfishly like the vamps, but just naturally, because you're empathic.

You are absorbing the energy of every single person you encounter. By the time you get to the end of your day, you could feel heavy, you could feel lazy, and you could feel drained, but not make the connection as to why. What happens when you soak something up with a sponge and then you just set it down? It gets nasty, it gets bacteria, it gets germs, it starts to smell. The same way you have to wring out a sponge to keep using it from day to day, you have to wring yourself out.

Not only are you not able to help anyone when you're soaked from the day before, but you're going to start leaking onto people as you go through your day. You'll start to notice that you're dripping out on everyone, you're in a foul mood, you have a nasty attitude, or you're snapping back at people that you don't mean to snap back at.

I was joking in my yoga class that it's like those Snickers commercials about not being yourself when you're hangry. This week's nugget is similar in that you're an empath. When your sponge is full, you are unable to give to anyone, especially yourself.

For me, one of the ways I wring myself out is with my yoga practice, both literally and figuratively. I fold and twist and sweat out the excess, then lie down at the end for savasana and wring out mentally too. We feel guilty about having "me" time, but that's not what we're doing, because you can't walk in your purpose if you look and feel like a three-day old sponge that has been sitting in the sink. I also find I can wring myself out in smaller ways, like walking my dog or walking out in my backyard barefoot. I try to find ways to wring out my mind and to wring out my body.

You're not going to be able to fix anything if you're so full of all of the yuck. Pay attention this week to when you feel lethargic, or have trouble getting out of bed. Notice when your attitude becomes negative and you are easily annoyed by things. All of these are signs that it's time to wring you out.

I know we talk about Self-Care Sunday, and wringing yourself out might not be a bubble bath. It might be going and sitting outside and watching the sunset. It might be a good book. There are lots of ways to bring yourself out. Journaling is a great way to wring yourself out—to get all the thoughts that are in your head out onto paper is a huge way to wring yourself out. It's going to be different for everybody.

I'm sharing some of what works for me, but it might be different for you; regardless, it has to be done on purpose. The mission, should you choose to accept it, is to figure out how to wring yourself out so that you can keep showing up every day. You have to be able to hold some healthier boundaries and recognize that your ability to give and to take care of others is dependent on your ability to give and take care of yourself. Move yourself to the front of the list. Wring it out.

What are the warning signs that you've been absorbing too much?

_____

_____

_____

_____

_____

_____

What self-care tasks help you recharge?

_____

_____

_____

_____

_____

_____

WEEK 51

SWIM WITH THE CURRENT.

It is safe to say that most of us have had some really bad things happen to us. I don't know anybody who hasn't experienced some kind of trauma, whether from abuse, grief, heartbreak, or war. When you go through something earth-shaking like trauma, whether you were a child or whether it was 2020, you get into fighter mode. Your survival instincts kick in and you become conditioned to show up every day ready for war. I learned how to be a fighter from birth. I was born into trauma, so all my developmental years were spent learning how to be a warrior.

These were valuable tools and skills that helped me get out of the bad situations my birth mother put me in. I clawed my way out of the crab bucket and now here I am, in another phase of my life. Those fighter skills were pivotal to me, but recently I have realized the negative side of being in fight mode. Because my programming is to fight, I make battles out of everything, including my blessings. I create problems where there aren't any, so I have something to overcome.

I'm going to say that again because this is going to be impactful for somebody. When you're trained to fight for everything, you turn everything into a fight. Some battles you fight in your life are going to be easier than others and you won't need your full armor. I found that I make them harder than they need to be because I'm planning for a worst-case scenario out of every situation I enter.

The skills you learn to survive are not the same skills that you're going to need to thrive. That means when you move out of survival mode into a different phase in your life, you can't keep bringing old ways of being and thinking. For me, it was specifically learning how to swim *with* the current. My whole life I've swum against the current, going upstream to get everything I needed, but swimming with the current feels foreign.

It feels uncomfortable and awkward. Why? Because it's fast. It's so incredibly fast it can feel hard to catch your breath. I can't control the speed and we already know how important control is in feeling safe.

If you're used to fighting for things, then you're used to digging your heels in, working hard, sweating, and bleeding to manifest the things that you want in your life. The long way around is the only way around. If something comes easy, you're going to question it. You're going to dismiss it and overthink it. You're going to make it a battle because you feel like it's supposed to be harder.

The phrase that rings in my ears: Nothing worth having comes easy. I know you have heard that, and I don't subscribe to that thought process anymore. I had to have a heart-to-heart with myself and ask: is that true?

It might have been true for me before, but is that true for me now? Or am I being my own worst enemy by bringing a battle to all my blessings? Could I swim with the current and could things be easier in my life if I stopped dragging my feet? If I stopped telling myself that it was too easy... if I stopped being a skeptic.

On a deeper note, I noticed that when a blessing came easily to me, it triggered my sense of worthiness. I don't deserve things unless I earn them with my blood, sweat, and tears. I could wear those battle wounds as proof that I am deserving of the thing I just achieved. This was easily the hardest mental block to get over. I am inherently deserving no matter what I have or how it came into my life. Programming like, I am only deserving of a raise if I work fifty hours a week and outperform every single person in the office.

Many of us are praying for abundance while simultaneously sabotaging everything coming into our lives. Not every environment is a war zone, so once you get out of the war zone, you must change your programming. The abundant chapter where you're thriving and living your best life in the flow of it all requires that you let go and trust. You have to let go of the past to lean into the future.

It's terrifying, the speed at which abundance can come into your life, because it's a foreign concept. If you've had to battle for every little scrap in your life, abundance feels scary and overwhelming. I'm feeling that as I'm moving into this new chapter of my life and things are just kind of falling in place, click, click, click. I want to make it hard. I want to slow things down because I need time to process it all, but abundance doesn't work like that. The flow doesn't work like that. The current will push you ahead if you learn to lean into it.

In what areas of your life are you dragging your feet?

_____

_____

_____

_____

_____

_____

What does abundance look like in your life?

_____

_____

_____

_____

_____

_____

WEEK 52

MY BOOK, NEW CHAPTER.

When I was younger, someone told me that when you are born you are assigned two angels, one who sees everything you do and one who writes it down. I don't know which one of the Abrahamic faiths this specifically stems from because Islam, Christianity, and Judaism all believe in angels. I've thought about this idea a lot over my lifetime.

It appeals to me because I believe that your entire journey is a story, a book of your life filled with chapter after chapter. The good, bad, and ugly of your time here on Earth are perfectly documented. If you're a reader, you know that the most compelling stories are filled with highs and lows.

The best books (or movies, if you're not a reader) have that moment when the hero or the star is down on their luck and is now suffering. We are inspired by their journey to overcome adversity. This part is usually accompanied by a musical montage in movies. The musical montage does a big disservice to the hard work required to be a cycle breaker or an overcomer in your own life.

The book of our lives is no different. We have chapters of suffering, and chapters of successes. Your story wouldn't be valuable if it didn't have any of that hardship. The hardship adds depth. That hardship is what makes it interesting. Trying to breeze through the healing process or skip the suffering does a disservice to our victory.

Healing, grief, and trauma are all messy and complex. There is no musical montage to help ease the suffering of these things or to speed them up. That is okay; it's allowed to take time. If you were in a car accident and broke your leg you wouldn't think to yourself, *why am I not healing faster*, but we do that with emotional and mental healing.

It's not just the desire to skip over the hard parts but the habit of re-reading old chapters. We become consumed with reading the hardship, it prevents us from writing the happy ending. That's so sad because the painful thing that happened to you has passed but you keep going back to sit in those ugly feelings. A wound can't heal if you keep picking at it.

I imagine my angels talking to each other—*oh, she wants to replay chapter 12 again*—and I think about how many pages of my story are nothing more than replays of previous chapters. What a boring story.

We all know someone who's trapped in the past. The ones reliving the good old days. Always talking about being the captain of the football team or winning homecoming queen. Every other sentence starts with: *back in my day...* They just keep replaying that old chapter. In their mind, that's the best it's ever going to get and now they're not even trying to make anything better out of their lives.

This pattern of replaying the past becomes self-inflicted suffering. Every minute you spend in the past is a minute lost on building your future. I want you to imagine that this week, you have a clean, fresh chapter to write in front of you. It's time to focus on your new chapter.

You are the author. You are the hero of your own story, so start acting like it. It's not over until you reach the end and you draw your last breath. Until then, you keep writing. Until then, you keep changing. Until then, you keep adding on until you get the victory story that you need.

Get out your pen and write down what you want this next chapter to look like and then start making it happen. I hope you all are inspired to take back your life, not just this week but as you conclude this journey with me. What comes next is up to you!

FINAL THOUGHTS

It is often said the only time you should look back is to see how far you've come. Take some time to look back through the pages. When you started this book, you had no idea what would resonate and what wouldn't. You filled these pages with your secrets, your pain, and your insecurities, but you also filled them with new ideas and hope.

Here you are now, a completely different person. You should be proud of yourself and know that I am proud of you. Many people will not make it this far. As the seasons of your life change, the way you look back at these nuggets will change as well. Remember that one of the key elements to growth is the ability to change your mind. Choose to remain flexible in your approach to life.

Healing is a journey, not a destination. Throughout the last fifty-two lessons, you have had an opportunity to self-reflect, ask hard questions, and look at your life through new eyes. Although we have come to the end of this book, your healing process should not end here. I hope you commit to keep going.

We cannot prevent the storms of life from coming and it is my true hope that when they do, you will feel more prepared to weather them because of the ideas and support this book offered you. I love you and am grateful you are a part of my tribe.

It has been a privilege to be on this journey with you. Thank you for trusting me and allowing me to inspire you. The light in me honors the light in you, and in this space, we are one.

Namaste, my friend!
Marie

Made in the USA
Middletown, DE
19 June 2022

67365397R00130